Employee Performance and Well-being

T0371799

This book provides recent inputs from the field of organizational behavior (OB) for enhancing employee performance and well-being, a key concern for managers today. It focuses on transformational leadership, organizational justice, organizational support, and workplace spirituality. The author outlines multiple dimensions of employee performance and five forms of employee well-being – physical, emotional, psychological, social, and spiritual. The book also presents an overview of the traditional approaches, and draws on relevant literature and empirical findings. It offers exercises from a practitioner's point of view to facilitate managerial actions and will serve as a practical application guide for managers.

This book will be of interest and use to students and researchers of human resource management, organizational behavior, management education, industrial and organizational psychology, corporate social responsibility and business ethics, as well as practicing HR managers and training managers.

Badrinarayan Shankar Pawar is Professor at the Indian Institute of Management Kozhikode, Kerala, India. Before this, he was Professor at the National Institute of Bank Management, Pune, Maharashtra, India. He completed his PhD from Oklahoma State University in 1996, with the highest possible cumulative grade point average of 4 out of 4 and received the membership of Phi Kappa Phi in recognition of his academic performance. He has published several research articles in leading journals and two books. Overall, for his published single-authored and co-authored research articles, the total of impact factors exceeds 27 and the number of citations received totals to over 1,600 as of September 2018. He has taught in the USA, Hong Kong, and India. His research interests include organizational citizenship behavior, transformational leadership, and workplace spirituality.

Employee Performance and Well-being

Leadership, Justice, Support, and Workplace Spirituality

Badrinarayan Shankar Pawar

Routledge
Taylor & Francis Group

LONDON AND NEW YORK

First published 2020
by Routledge
2 Park Square, Milton Park, Abingdon, Oxon OX14 4RN

and by Routledge
605 Third Avenue, New York, NY 10017

First issued in paperback 2021

Routledge is an imprint of the Taylor & Francis Group, an informa business

© 2020 Badrinarayan Shankar Pawar

British Library Cataloguing-in-Publication Data
A catalogue record for this book is available from the British Library

Library of Congress Cataloging-in-Publication Data
Names: Pawar, Badrinarayan Shankar, 1962– author.
Title: Employee Performance and Well-being : Leadership, Justice, Jupport, and Workplace Spirituality / Badrinarayan Shankar Pawar.
Description: Abingdon, Oxon ; New York, NY : Routledge, 2019. | Includes bibliographical references.
Identifiers: LCCN 2018056794 | ISBN 9781138082700 (hardback : alk. paper) | ISBN 9780429244193 (e-book)
Subjects: LCSH: Personnel management. | Performance. | Organizational behavior.
Classification: LCC HF5549 .P298 2019 | DDC 658.3/14—dc23
LC record available at https://lccn.loc.gov/2018056794

Typeset in Sabon
by Apex CoVantage, LLC

ISBN 13: 978-0-367-78594-9 (pbk)
ISBN 13: 978-1-138-08270-0 (hbk)

I dedicate this book to my late father, Mr. Shankar Hari Pawar, and my late mother, Mrs. Chandrabhaga Shankar Pawar, who made several sacrifices for inspiring and helping me to obtain education and to use it in the noble service. I dedicate this book to them for also the amazingly lofty standards of spirituality, morality, idealism, purposiveness, dedication, and courage they practiced and through which they provided to me many ideals to pursue in my own life. This book is dedicated to them with gratitude, because my education and life is their property and gift to me. There are several individuals, who cannot be identified by name, who suffered because of me. I dedicate this book to them with my prayers to them for forgiveness.

"A river cleanses and nourishes others but it merges itself in the ocean. The Sun dispels the world's darkness and opens temples of illumination naturally in its daily round. In the same manner, always liberating the bonded, rescuing the drowned, fulfilling the aspirations of the distressed, and doing the work for other's good takes one to the Self. As trees and creepers let go their fruits, let go the fruits of one's accomplishments." (An approximate translated interpretation of Verses 199-202 in Chapter 16, p. 468 and Verse 129 in Chapter 12, p. 312 of Shri Dnyaneshwari which is a part of the elaboration by Saint Shri Dnyaneshwar ji of Verse 3 in Chapter 16 and Verse 11 in Chapter 12 of Shri Bhagwad Geeta). Reflecting this guidance which my mother Smt. Chandrabhaga Bai also exemplified in her life, the work on this book is an attempt to do some good by providing illumination and I pray that I endeavour to let go its fruits.

Reference

Shri Dnyaneshwari. 2016. D. Tandale (Ed.). Amol Prakashan: Pune, India

Contents

Figures

Preface

In my academic career as a researcher and teacher in the area of organizational behavior (OB), I had an urge to contribute to the managerial practice by facilitating managers' constructive actions in organizations. I realized that two of the main objectives for managers are to obtain high levels of performance from employees and to provide a high level of well-being to employees. From the OB body of knowledge that I was familiar with, I identified certain organizational features and actions that seemed to be relevant for enhancing both employee performance and employee well-being. In particular, I identified four OB topics – transformational leadership, organizational justice, organizational support, and workplace spirituality – that were relatively recent and in which a reasonable amount of empirical evidence was available, which suggested that these aspects can contribute to enhancing both employee performance and well-being. I had studied each of these topics during the various phases and in varying degrees over the course of my academic research work spanning about 25 years. In a few of these areas, I had also done and published research.

From the early part of my research career, I was drawn to such OB research areas as employees' organizational citizenship behaviors and transformational leadership. In the course of my research, I also studied and used inputs from the areas such as organizational justice and organizational support. When I began to reflect on the possible common underlying theme in my getting drawn to these OB areas, I discovered that most of these areas had a humanistic orientation in that they sought to do something positive to employees and to organizations and to induce positive responses from employees. I also realized that most of these areas also focus on inducing employees to transcend their self-interests. Thus, at some point in my academic career, I pointed out the common element of self-interest transcendence in the areas of transformational leadership, organizational justice, organizational support, workplace spirituality, and employees' organizational citizenship behavior (Pawar, 2009). In the same work, I also noted that these areas reflect a humanistic orientation.

Thus, multiple aspects, such as my urge to contribute through OB knowledge to the managerial practice, my inclination to use the scientific body of OB knowledge in this process, and my affinity to the humanistic areas of OB, guided the activities of teaching, training, and research in the later part of my academic career. For example, I designed and singlehandedly taught a training program on enhancing employee performance and well-being through leadership, justice, support, and spirituality. I taught the program a number of times, and from the feedback of the participants in this training program, I learned that the program provides useful inputs to managers for enhancing employee performance and well-being. However, the benefits of such a training program can be availed only by those managers who attend the program.

Thus, in order to provide the benefits of the inputs of leadership, justice, support, and workplace spirituality for enhancing employee performance and well-being to a larger number of practicing managers and also to the management students who are prospective managers, I felt it would be useful to make a book on these aspects available to practicing managers and management students. Partly from this thinking, the task of writing this present book was taken up.

This book, thus, is an outcome of my personal affinity for the humanistic aspects of organizational life and of the OB as a scientific body of knowledge, my urge to make a contribution to managerial practice through the application of the scientific body of OB knowledge, and the evolution of my teaching, training, and research over my academic career. I hope that this book will be useful to both practicing managers and also to management students who are getting educated for being managers.

As reflected in the above, this book has evolved from my exposure, over several years, to some knowledge areas of organizational behaviour, my reflection, and my teaching and training. As a result, in my expressions in the book, inputs coming from the literature, from my reflection, and from teaching and training activities are likely to have got blended together. Thus, it is likely that some literature works influenced my thinking and shaped my expressions in this book but I was not consciously aware, during the process of my work on this book, of the connection of my expressions in this book to such literature works. These aspects may have led to some instances where inadvertent omission in citing some relevant literature works may have occurred. For such instances, if any, I seek forgiveness from all and pray that the readers and scholars will point out to me such instances, if any, which they may note so that I can rectify such inadvertent omissions in the future editions of this book.

Reference

Pawar, B. S. 2009. Some of the recent organizational behavior concepts as precursors to workplace spirituality. *Journal of Business Ethics*, 88: 245–261.

Acknowledgments

I gratefully acknowledge the help I received in a part of my early education from various sources. While my thinking and work on the themes in this book evolved over quite a few years, the initial conceptualization and integration of some of these themes occurred during my period of work at the Indian Institute of Management Kozhikode between about the middle of 2008 until early 2014 – I gratefully acknowledge the support I received there. I gratefully acknowledge that considerable part of my work on this book took place during a part of my employment with the National Institute of Bank Management, Pune, India. I remain grateful to National Institute of Bank Management, Pune for having made is feasible for me to have the time to do my considerable work on this book there during years 2017 and 2018. There are several individuals who supported and helped me during my education and academic career. While it is difficult to identify all of my benefactors individually, the following names come to my mind most readily: Dr. Kenneth K. Eastman, the late Dr. Wayne Meinhart, Dr. Pradip Khandwalla, Dr. Vijaya Sherry Chand, Dr. Mathukutty M. Monippally, Dr. S. Krishnamoorthy, Dr. Sanjay Banerji, Dr. Debashis Chatterjee, Dr. K. Unnikrishnan Nair, and Dr. Sumit Ghosh. I acknowledge their support with a sense of gratitude.

The following figures have been reproduced in this book with appropriate permissions from the author's other published works:

Chapter 3

Figure 3.1 Interconnected effects of leadership, justice, support, and workplace spirituality on employee performance and well-being (Reprinted with permission from Elsevier: B. S. Pawar (2015),

Enhancing research-teaching link in organizational behavior: Illustration through an actual example, *The International Journal of Management Education*, 13: 326–336. Reproduced and adapted from p. 331.)

Chapter 8

Figure 8.2 Some ways of enhancing employee experiences of workplace spirituality (Reprinted with permission from Springer Nature: B. S. Pawar (2009), Workplace spirituality facilitation: A comprehensive model, *Journal of Business Ethics*, 90(3): 375–386. Reproduced from p. 382.)

Chapter 9

Figure 9.2 How leadership, justice, support, and workplace spirituality can be applied with other organizational behavior interventions (Reprinted with permission from Springer Nature: B. S. Pawar (2013), A proposed model of organizational behavior aspects for employee performance and well-being, *Applied Research in Quality of Life*, 8(3): 339–359. Reproduced and adapted from p. 349.)

Introduction

Employee performance and employee well-being are two of the main desirable outcomes for an organization. Therefore, managers need to take actions for enhancing employee performance and well-being in their organizations. They may receive guidance for such actions from various sources such as their past experience, their intuition, and the recommendations coming from their higher authorities. For managers, another source of guidance for their actions is the scientific body of knowledge on factors that can enhance employee performance and well-being. This book seeks to provide inputs, based on the scientific body of knowledge, to managers for enhancing employee performance and employee well-being.

In Chapter 1, the phenomenon of employee performance is described. The chapter points out that employees' overall performance is much broader than only task performance that focuses on the quantity and quality of work produced. It points out that contextual performance or employees' organizational citizenship behavior is also an important part of employees' overall performance. Chapter 1 also discusses other components of employees' overall performance. Thus, this chapter can help managers broaden their view of and understand various components of employees' overall performance.

Chapter 2 describes employee well-being. It outlines what employee well-being is and why it is important. It then describes five forms of well-being: physical, emotional, psychological, social, and spiritual. It also outlines that well-being is not only the absence of mental ill-health or stress, but that it requires the presence of positive mental health. Chapter 2 also contains a few exercises to facilitate an experiential understanding and application of some relevant aspects of employee well-being.

Chapter 3 outlines that employee performance and employee well-being are the two desired outcomes for an organization. It also describes that while an organization needs to simultaneously attain high level of employee performance and well-being, it may be possible that only one of these is being emphasized at the cost of the other one. Chapter 3 points out that, despite challenges, it is feasible for an organization to have high levels of both employee performance and employee well-being. It then indicates that this book focuses on four input areas, namely transformational leadership, organizational justice, organizational support, and workplace spirituality, for enhancing employee performance and employee well-being. It explains some of the distinctive positive features of these action areas.

Chapter 4 provides a brief overview of the some of the traditional approaches to enhancing employee performance and well-being. The four main action areas – transformational leadership, organizational justice, organizational support, and workplace spirituality – for enhancing employee performance and well-being covered in this book are of relatively recent origin as scientific topics in the organizational behavior (OB) field. Some of the other approaches that preceded the emergence of these four action areas are referred to here as traditional approaches, and a few of these are briefly outlined only to provide a backdrop against which the four main action areas covered in the book can be understood. The traditional approaches outlined in this chapter are the scientific management approach, the human relations approach, participative management, job enrichment, the job characteristics model, goal-setting, and work teams or self-managed teams.

Chapter 5 describes the first of the main four action areas – transformational leadership – for enhancing employee performance and well-being covered in the book. It describes what leadership is and why leadership is required in an organization. It then outlines various forms of leadership and provides a detailed description of transformational leadership. It describes specific behaviors included in practicing transformational leadership and illustrates them through examples. Chapter 5 also outlines the likely effects of transformational leadership and indicates some of the supportive empirical evidence. The chapter also includes exercises to facilitate reflection on and application of some of the aspects in practicing transformational leadership.

Chapter 6 focuses on the action area of organizational justice. It describes justice in general and its importance in human life. It then describes justice in the specific setting of organizations, which is termed as organizational justice. It then describes distributive justice, procedural justice, and interactional justice as three forms of organizational justice. For each of these forms of organizational justice, Chapter 6 describes its basic features, explains why employees are likely to pay attention to it, outlines some of the likely consequences of it, and describes some of the actions that can help enhance it in an organization. This chapter also includes exercises to facilitate reflection on and application in a workplace of some of the aspects of organizational justice.

Chapter 7 is on the action area of organizational support. It describes the nature of employee beliefs of organizational support. It outlines why and how employees develop beliefs of organizational support. It describes how employee beliefs of organizational support influence employees' feelings, motivation, and actions. It outlines some of the relevant empirical evidence on the outcomes of and on the factors influencing employee beliefs of organizational support. Chapter 7 also includes exercises to facilitate reflection on and application in the workplace of employee beliefs of organizational support.

Chapter 8 covers the action area of workplace spirituality. It describes spirituality as a human need. It then outlines the nature of the human need for spirituality in terms of seeking to transcend oneself or to go beyond oneself and seeking to connect to and contribute to others. It then describes workplace spirituality. Chapter 8 also outlines some of the outcomes of workplace spirituality, including the outcomes of employee performance and well-being. It then describes some of the factors that can influence employee experiences of workplace spirituality. This chapter also includes an exercise to facilitate the application of workplace spirituality to an actual work unit.

Chapter 9, the last chapter, outlines some reflections on implementing actions based on the four action areas – transformational leadership, organizational justice, organizational support, and workplace spirituality – for enhancing employee performance and well-being. It describes the value of research-based inputs provided in this book for managers for enhancing employee performance and well-being. It also provides some directions for implementing actions as well as for implementing interconnected actions for improving the level of transformational leadership, organizational justice, organizational support, and workplace spirituality for enhancing employee performance and well-being.

Chapter I

Employee performance

An organization's requirement from employees

Exercise I: Assessment of employee performance in a work unit

This exercise is to be completed before reading the chapter. It can facilitate application of the "performance" aspect to the actual work units.

Directions

Before you read this chapter, do the following exercise for your organization. Using a separate sheet, write down your responses to each of the following questions.

1. Describe what is meant by "employee performance" in your organization.
2. List five different jobs/roles in your organization.
3. From the above list, for *any one job*:

   a. Describe the job briefly.
   b. Describe the employee behaviors that are regarded as positive performance in that job.
   c. Describe how adequately the employee behaviors described above completely reflect positive performance in that job.
   d. List what other employee behaviors need to be included to completely assess employee performance in that job.
   e. Explain why these additional employee behaviors need to be included to completely describe employee performance in that job.

f.   Describe how a more complete view of employee performance in this job may affect (hurt/benefit) your organization.

After you read the chapter, reflect on how adequately your responses to the above items described employee performance.

Exercise 2: Appreciate employee performance through example scenarios

In the following hypothetical examples, two work units A and B are described. A work unit could be a department in a hospital where employees are doctors, nurses, ward staff, and other support staff; a library in an academic institute; or a bank branch where employees could be a branch manager, officers, clerical staff, and support staff. Now consider a bank branch as a work unit in the following examples.

Organizational unit A

Consider the following organizational unit A.

In unit A, which is a bank branch, employees mostly provide advance notice if they need to take a leave. In the bank branch, employees come on time. Employees help those coworkers who are new or have some family-related difficulties. This help could be through sharing the coworkers' workload or by listening to their problems and providing empathy or advice to them. Employees exert a high level of effort on their jobs and persist when they face difficulties. For example, if an employee does not know the procedures to complete a transaction requested by a customer, rather than turn the customer away to a higher-level officer, the employee could quickly ask someone about the correct procedures and use them to complete the transaction. Employees avoid creating problems for other coworkers. For example, an employee working at one of the counters would avoid making long personal phone calls during working hours, because that would slow down his/her work and increase the work for the employees at other counters rendering similar service. Employees read circulars and notices that might affect their work in the branch. Employees usually tolerate small inconveniences such as overhead cooling fans or air conditioners not functioning properly.

Organizational unit B

Consider the following organizational unit B.

In unit B, which is a bank branch, employees remain absent without providing advance notice and fill in the leave application form only when they return to work after the absence days. In the bank branch, quite a few employees frequently come late. Employees do not help those coworkers who are new or have some family-related difficulties. Thus, for example, employees will not share the heavy workload of an employee and thus the employee with heavy workload would not receive help or employees will not listen to a coworker's personal difficulties or provide him/her empathy or advice. Employees do not exert a high level of effort on their jobs and do not persist when they face difficulties. For example, if an employee does not know the procedures to complete a transaction requested by a customer, rather than quickly asking someone about the correct procedures and using them to complete the transaction, he/she will turn the customer away to a higher-level officer. Employees do not take care to avoid creating problems for other coworkers. For example, an employee working at one of the counters would make long personal phone calls during working hours while not considering that this would slow down his/her work and increase the work for the employees at other counters rendering similar service. Employees do not read circulars and notices that might affect their work in the branch. Employees usually make noise about small inconveniences such as overhead cooling fans or air conditioners not functioning properly.

Now answer the following questions based on the previously outlined descriptions of work unit A and work unit B.

1. Suppose you have a choice to be in charge of either unit A or unit B. Which of the two work units would you choose to be in charge of?
2. Provide justification for your choice of work unit to be in charge of.
3. Which of the two work units would be more productive?
4. For the work unit mentioned by you in response to question 3, provide an explanation of why you think it would be more productive.
5. Explain how the employee behaviors and contributions in work unit A are in addition to employee performance of their producing the work of adequate quantity and quality.

Employee performance: An important objective of organizations

The origins of industrial organizations can be traced to the industrial revolution. One of the prescriptions emerging from the industrial revolution period was to adopt the division of labor. The division of labor principle suggests that a job needs to be divided into a number of tasks, and one or more tasks need to be assigned to each employee in such a way that each employee does a particular fragment of the overall job and hence becomes a specialist in it. Considerable gain in employee performance was one of the claimed benefits of the application of the division of labor principle.

The performance gains associated with the division of labor principle can be seen from the example of comparing two approaches to doing the job of paper pin manufacturing. In one approach to the job, each employee did all the tasks associated with the job, such as straightening the wire, cutting the wire, and sharpening the wire piece. In the alternative approach, the tasks associated with the pin manufacturing job were divided among employees such that one employee straightened the wire, another one cut the wire, another one sharpened the wire piece end, and so on. It was observed that employee performance measured as the number of pins produced per employee was considerably higher in the latter approach than in the former approach. Specifically, Wren (1987, p. 30) notes that "Adam Smith ... cited the example of the pin-makers who, when each performed a limited operation, could produce 48,000 pins per day, whereas one unspecialized worker could do no more than twenty pins per day." Thus, the division of labor principle can be seen as a suggestion for employee performance enhancement by arranging the job performance tasks in a particular way.

In the early period of modern industrial organizations around the beginning of the 20th century, the scientific management approach proposed by F. W. Taylor and his associates contained various techniques. These included time and motion study, standardization of work methods, specialization, assignment of task to individual employees, specification of a production target or goal to each employee, provision of bonus or monetary incentive for high performance, scientific selection of employees, and provision of training to employees (Locke, 1982; Taylor, 1911/2007). Of these techniques, the specialization technique reflects division of labor, because this technique involves making each employee do a specialized part of the overall job. The scientific management approach to doing jobs also demonstrated considerable improvement in productivity (e.g., Taylor, 1911/2007).

In contemporary industrial organizations, employee performance remains one of the main concerns. An example of this concern is the view of Fry and Slocum (2008) that performance or profit is one of the greatest challenges faced by contemporary leaders.

Thus, employee performance has been an objective of organizations in the period of industrial revolution, of scientific management that emerged around the early part of the 20th century, and of contemporary modern organizations. In light of the importance of employee performance for organizations, it is relevant to consider what employee performance is. Thus, the concept of employee performance is described below.

Employee performance: What is it?

Employee performance may be generally viewed as the level of relevant output produced by an employee. For example, performance of a teacher could be assessed in terms of the number of hours taught by the teacher and in terms of feedback from students. In this example, the number of hours taught by a teacher reflects the quantity of work produced, and the nature of teaching feedback received from students reflects the quality of work produced. As another example, performance of a bank cashier could be assessed by considering the combination of the number of cash-dispensing transactions and the number of cash receipt transactions completed over a certain period, the average time taken to serve a customer, and the quality of service provided to the customers during their transactions. This is the traditional view of employee performance.

Two features should be noted concerning this traditional view of employee performance, which focuses on the quantity and quality of outputs produced on a job. First, it focuses on an employee's performance on the job or task. Therefore, it is actually an employee's task performance or on-the-job performance rather than an employee's overall performance. An employee's overall performance includes, in addition to the employee's task performance, extra-role performance or contextual performance, such as taking extra responsibility, helping coworkers, and making innovative suggestions.

Second, the traditional view of employee performance focuses on the task results attained by an employee rather than the behaviors of the employee. However, employee performance can also be viewed as an evaluative judgment as to the extent to which an employee's behaviors have facilitated or impaired the attainment of the organization's goals (Motowidlo, Borman, and Schmitt, 1997). According to this view of employee performance, an employee's behaviors such as ignoring quality checks, working slow on the job, and using inappropriate raw materials impair the attainment of an organization's goals. Hence, the evaluative judgment of such behaviors is that of negative, poor, or low performance. Further, according to this view of employee performance, employee behaviors such as meticulously doing quality checks, working at the required or higher pace on the job, and using appropriate raw materials facilitate the attainment of the organization's goals. Hence, the evaluative judgment of such behaviors is that of positive, good, or high performance. The employee behaviors forming the negative, poor, or low performance are likely to attain poor results in terms of quantity and quality of work produced, whereas the employee behaviors forming the positive, good, or high performance are likely to attain good results. Thus, the view of performance as an evaluative judgment of employee behaviors in terms of the extent to which the behaviors facilitate or impair the attainment of an organization's goals indirectly reflects the results attainment and provides a more detailed view of employee performance than does the view provided by focusing only on the results.

The two features outlined above indicate that employee performance needs to be viewed as an evaluative judgment of the extent to which an employee's behaviors facilitate or impair the attainment of an organization's goals. Further, not only the employee's on-the-job or task-related behaviors but also extra-role behaviors need to be included in assessing employee performance (e.g., Motowidlo et al., 1997). In the literature, the task performance part is also referred to as in-role performance or on-the-job performance, while the extra-role performance is referred to as contextual performance (Motowidlo et al., 1997) or organizational citizenship behaviors (e.g., Organ, 1988).

A closer look at employees' contextual performance

The discussion above indicates that an employee's performance refers to the judgment about the extent to which the employee's in-role or on-the-job or task behaviors and extra-role behaviors facilitate the attainment of an organization's goals. Thus, an employee's overall performance involves a judgment based on both an employee's in-role or task behaviors and an employee's extra-role or non-task behaviors.

The judgment about the extent to which an employee's non-task or extra-role behaviors facilitate or impede an organization's goal attainment is referred to as contextual performance. Formally, employee contextual performance is defined as those behaviors of employees that nourish or support the social and psychological context in which the work occurs (Motowidlo et al., 1997). Another label used in the literature to refer to similar behaviors is organizational citizenship behaviors (OCBs) (e.g., Organ, 1988). OCBs refer to an employee's behaviors that have certain features. These behaviors are not specified as a part of the employee's formal role, an employee performing these behaviors does not seek immediate rewards from performing them, and these behaviors benefit the organization (e.g., Organ, 1988). Based on these features of OCBs, OCBs can be referred to as extra-role, non-reward-seeking, and organizationally beneficial employee behaviors (e.g., Organ, 1988).

A review of OCB research (Podsakoff, MacKenzie, Paine, and Bacharach, 2000) indicates that there are several perspectives, each containing one list of OCB categories, outlining multiple OCB categories. Similarly, Coleman and Borman (2000, p. 28–29) indicate 14 different works in the literature outlining various OCBs which they labeled as "citizenship performance behaviors." Examples of employee OCBs include helping new coworkers at work, helping those coworkers who are facing difficulties such as personal illness or family issues, voluntarily taking extra responsibilities, complying with organizational norms and being tolerant of small inconveniences without making a big noise about them (e.g., Coleman and Borman, 2000; Moorman and Blakely, 1995; Smith, Organ, and Near, 1983; Williams and Anderson, 1991). These examples of extra-role behaviors reflect positive contextual performance or the OCB of an employee. Just as OCBs or positive extra-role performance reflect an employee's positive contributions to organizational goal attainment, there can be negative extra-role performance or negative contextual performance (e.g., Eastman and Pawar, 2005; Rotundo and Sackett, 2002) of an employee, and an employee's refraining from them can be viewed as positive extra-role performance. In light of this, a brief overview of anti-OCBs is provided below.

Negative contextual performance

Just as employees perform positive extra-role behaviors in the form of OCBs, some employees can potentially perform negative extra-role behaviors. These behaviors may include destroying an organization's property, spreading foul rumors about the organization, and taking longer than permitted breaks (e.g., Robinson and Bennett, 1995). Such behaviors reflect low or negative performance of an employee because they impair the attainment of an organization's goals. In the literature, these behaviors have been given labels such as deviant workplace behaviors (e.g., Robinson and Bennett, 1995), antisocial behaviors (Robinson and O'Leary-Kelly, 1998), and negative behaviors (Eastman and Pawar, 2005).

Within the negative behaviors, various specific forms of negative behaviors can occur. For example, negative behaviors can be minor or serious and could be against organizational members or the organization itself (Robinson and Bennett, 1995). Minor deviance against organizational members can include gossiping about an employee, while serious deviance against organizational members could include placing a coworker in an unsafe situation (Robinson and Bennett, 1995). Minor deviance against an organization can include leaving the workplace before the scheduled closing time, while serious deviance against an organization can include employees' theft (Robinson and Bennett, 1995).

While the previous sections illustrated various positive and negative forms of employee performance, there are other employee behavior categories that can also facilitate the attainment of an organization's goal and hence can constitute positive performance of an employee. Two forms of such behavior – timely arrival at work and maintaining organizational membership – are discussed below.

Timely arrival at work

An employee's lateness in arriving at work can be detrimental to the attainment of an organization's goals and hence can constitute an employee's negative performance. For example, Robinson and Bennett (1995, p. 571) included late arrival at work as one of the behavioral indicators of behaviors that are detrimental to an organization and contrarily, punctual behavior is taken as indicator of OCB in Smith et al. (1983, p. 657). As an illustration, consider the late arrival of a professor for commencing his/her early morning class.

All students in the class will remain idle; or worse still, they can create clamor and disturb other classes with their loud conversations. Further, with such lateness of a professor, the importance of sincerity and discipline in the minds of students could be lowered. If several professors arrive late for starting their classes and if this happens reasonably frequently, students could also start arriving late for their classes, lower their respect for the professors and for the institute, and engage in other forms of indiscipline-expressing behaviors. This example illustrates that the late arrival behavior of professors can impair the academic organization's goal attainment and hence constitutes a negative performance of professors.

Another example can also illustrate the negative performance emerging from the lack of timely arrival at work. Consider an organization in the airline industry. The airline organization may have a specific staff member in the aircraft maintenance crew who needs to inspect an aircraft's machinery before the aircraft can fly with passengers on board.

Consider a situation in which such a staff member arrives late for his/her regularly scheduled inspection of an aircraft, which is scheduled to fly shortly. If a standby staff is not available for the job, the aircraft may need to either fly without its being inspected or fly late, thus possibly delaying the flight for several passengers who may be traveling on that aircraft. Such repeated instances of late flights of an airline organization can induce negative customer reactions against the airline and eventually affect the business of the airline organization. This example also illustrates how a lack of timely arrival of employees constitutes negative performance.

If the above two examples are viewed from another angle, a professor's timely arrival for classes and the aircraft inspection staff's timely arrival for the aircraft inspection constitute the professor's and inspection staff's positive performance. Thus, timely attendance of work is one category of employees' positive performance.

Regular work attendance

An employee's regular attendance at work also constitutes his/her positive performance. Rotundo and Sackett's (2002, p. 67) summary of various descriptions of performance lists low absenteeism as one aspect of performance. Better-than-required attendance and providing notice of the likely absence are included as behavioral indicators of the organizational citizenship behavior measure of Smith, Organ, and Near (1983, p. 657), and Williams and Anderson (1991, p. 606). An employee's regular work attendance can benefit an organization. As an illustration, consider the following example of a nurse who works for a small private hospital. The hospital is small and has a few in-house doctors and nurses. For performing surgeries, the hospital invites experienced surgeons from other hospitals on an as-needed basis and pays them on an hourly basis for their time spent at the hospital. The nurse, because of his/her specialized experience, can assist surgeons during the surgery in the operations theater. None of the remaining few nurses can do this job because they do not have adequate experience of assisting in the surgery in the operations theater. On a particular day, a serious surgery is scheduled at 8:00 a.m., which is the hospital's morning shift's opening time. The hospital has hired the services of three experienced surgeons from other hospitals who have already arrived at the hospital, and the relatives of the patient on whom the surgery is to be performed are eager and anxious that the surgery be performed immediately.

However, while it is a little past 8:00 a.m., the nurse who is to do the work of assisting in the surgery room does not arrive at work. When the hospital staff contacts him/her on the phone to make inquiries, the nurse expresses that he/she cannot attend work that day because of a difficult situation in his/her family that day. At that time, the hospital has only a few options, such as obtain another specialist nurse from some other hospital or require another nurse, who may not be adequately capable of assisting in the surgery room, to do the job of assisting in the surgery room that day, or cancel the surgery and reschedule it for a later day. Each of these three options has adverse implications for the hospital. Specifically, the option of canceling the surgery that day and rescheduling it for a later day may require the surgeons to be paid because they have already arrived at the hospital, their time is wasted by the hospital by keeping them idle, and they could have earned some compensation if they had spent the same time doing surgery at another hospital. Further, the surgeons may need to be called at a later day, and working which day is convenient for all external surgeons may have its own difficulties. Dealing with the relatives of the patient who were eager and anxious that the surgery be performed immediately could be a difficult task. If such instances are repeated a few times, the hospital's service and image could be adversely affected.

In the above example, the nurse's nonattendance adversely affects the hospital's goal attainment and thus constitutes negative performance. Viewed from another angle, employees' regular attendance constitutes their positive performance.

Maintaining organizational membership

An employee's remaining with an organization also constitutes positive employee performance. Rotundo and Sackett's (2002, p. 67) summary of various descriptions of performance lists remaining with the organization as one aspect of performance. Similarly, "staying with the organization" even in difficult circumstances is identified as one of the citizenship performance behaviors in Colman and Borman (2000, p. 29). When an employee quits an organization, the organization's workflow can, in principle, be disrupted. In certain situations, an organization has to look for a replacement for the employee who has quit. A suitable replacement may not be immediately feasible or obtaining a suitable replacement on an immediate basis may have some extra cost. When a new employee is freshly recruited as a replacement, there is the cost of recruitment, selection, socialization, and training. Further, the newly recruited employee may take quite some time before he/she becomes fully productive. In addition, an employee's quitting can cause socio-emotional loss to his/her coworkers. Thus, an employee's remaining with the organization can avoid such negative consequences for the organization and thereby make positive contributions to the attainment of the organization's goals. Hence, remaining with the organization constitutes one positive performance component of an employee's overall performance.

Overall performance of an employee

As described earlier, when an employee has good performance, it reflects a judgment that the employee's behaviors facilitate the attainment of an organization's goals. On-the-job performance, task performance, or in-role performance are different labels referring to the extent to which an employee's job-related behaviors facilitate the attainment of an organization's goals. Contextual performance, positive extra-role behaviors, or organizational citizenship behaviors reflect another form of an employee's positive performance. Refraining from anti-OCBs, or workplace deviant behaviors or workplace antisocial behaviors, also reflects an employee's positive performance. Various works (e.g., Eastman and Pawar, 2005; Motowidlo et al., 1997; Rotundo and Sacket, 2002) have included two or more of the above performance dimensions in describing employee performance.

Regularly attending work, arriving at work on time, and remaining with an organization also constitute parts of an employee's positive performance or good performance. An employee's overall performance consists of these several forms of employee behaviors. Thus, an employee's overall good performance requires all the above aspects, and an absence or undesirably low level of any of them can lower an employee's overall performance. Some of these multiple dimensions of employee performance are depicted in Figure 1.1.

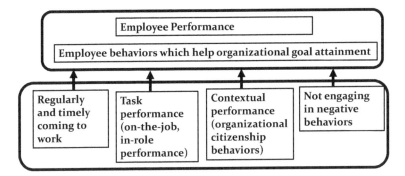

Figure 1.1 Dimensions of employee performance

Source: Partly based on various works including Motowidlo et al. (1997), Eastman and Pawar (2005), Rotundo and Sackett (2002), and the preceding description in this chapter.

Revisit and reflect on your work in Exercise 1

In Exercise 1 at the beginning of this chapter, you would have described your view of what an employee's performance is. Now, in light of the description of various dimensions of employee performance provided in the preceding part of this chapter and depicted in Figure 1.1, reflect on how adequate your view of employee performance was before reading this chapter. Also reflect on how it is beneficial for you as a manager to broaden your view of employee performance to include the multiple dimensions of employee performance described in the preceding part of this chapter and depicted in Figure 1.1.

Are non-task-related aspects of employee performance important?

Earlier in the chapter and in Figure 1.1, it is pointed out that employees' non-task-related performance dimensions, such as contextual performance, are also a part of employees' overall performance. Thus, a point to consider is how important the non-task-related performance or contextual performance is. Two forms of empirical evidence from research indicate that non-task-related aspects of employee performance are important.

The first category of empirical evidence indicates that supervisors' overall performance ratings of their subordinates are significantly influenced by the non-task-related aspects of employee performance or contextual performance (Borman and Motowidlo, 1997). Some of the research on this aspect also indicates that the impact of the subordinates' contextual performance on the overall performance rating assigned by the supervisors is nearly equal to the impact of task performance on on-the-job performance (Borman and Motowidlo, 1997).

The second category of evidence indicates that work teams and work units in which employees perform higher organizational citizenship behaviors, which is a behavior category similar to the contextual performance category, tend to have higher levels of performance (Podsakoff and MacKenzie, 1997). This evidence comes from units such as paper mill work crews, pharmaceutical sales teams, insurance agency units, and limited menu restaurants (Podsakoff and MacKenzie, 1997).

This empirical evidence and the explanations provided earlier in this chapter suggest that employees' organizational citizenship behaviors or contextual performance are important. The importance of employees' organizational citizenship behaviors or contextual performance can also be understood by closely considering the differences in the non-task-related performance in a manager's best and worst subordinates. Thus, Exercise 3, which will be done at the end of this chapter, may help you see more closely that the non-task-related aspects of employee performance are important. Before you do Exercise 3, revisit your work on Exercise 2 from the earlier part of this chapter.

Revisit and reflect on your work on Exercise 2

Now, again read the descriptions of work unit A and work unit B provided in Exercise 2 "Appreciate Employee Performance through Example Scenarios" in the earlier part of this chapter and also read your answers to the questions in that exercise. In Exercise 2, you were required to make a choice of work unit A or work unit B for being in charge of. You were also required to provide justification for your choice, to indicate which of the two work units would be more effective, and to explain the reasons why one of these two work units would be more productive.

It is quite likely that you chose to be in charge of work unit A. This is not surprising, and most managers would make the same choice. Upon again reading the descriptions of work units A and B in the earlier part of this chapter, in your view now, which of the two work units has a higher level of employees' organizational citizenship behaviors (OCB) or contextual performance? It is clear that work unit A has higher levels of OCB. Thus, you chose to be in charge of a work unit that has a high level of OCB. Now read the justification you provided for your choice of work unit A. Your justifications are likely to refer directly or indirectly to the many positive behaviors or OCBs of employees in work unit A. From your responses in Exercise 2, you may realize that it is beneficial and hence desirable for a manager to ensure high levels of OCB in his/her work unit.

Now, read your answer to the Exercise 2 question on which of the work units would be more productive. Your answer would have indicated that work unit A would be more productive. This is consistent with the empirical evidence described in the earlier part of this chapter that work units having higher levels of employee OCB tend to be more productive. Thus, your thinking, reflected in your responses to Exercise 2 questions, is consistent with the empirical evidence from research (e.g., Podsakoff and MacKenzie, 1997).

Read the reasons you provided for explaining why you think work unit A would be more productive. These reasons are likely to include that in work unit A, individual employee productivity level would be high, unit morale level is likely to be high, and supervisors can focus their efforts on improving their work units as employees will train, support, and help each other. Such reasons provided by you in response to the last question of Exercise 2 are similar to the explanations from the literature (e.g., Podsakoff and MacKenzie, 1997).

Thus, your individual thinking and the explanations provided in the literature both suggest similar reasons why employee OCBs in a work unit make the work unit more productive.

Finally, read the explanations you provided in response to the last question of Exercise 2. From your explanations and from the nature of employee behaviors contained in the description of work unit A, you would see that employee behaviors in work unit A are different from employee behaviors of working to produce task performance of adequate quantity and quality. As the employee behaviors in work unit A are employee OCBs, you will realize that employee OCBs are different from employee task performance and that employee OCBs can take many forms, such as helping coworkers, tolerating small inconveniences, and avoiding problems for coworkers. These examples of employee OCBs indicate that an employee's OCB may not enhance his/her task performance in terms of quantity and quality of work produced by him/her, but that it might contribute to work unit productivity in other ways.

From your revisit to and reflection on Exercise 2, you would have realized the following. First, as a manager, it is desirable for you to have high levels of employee OCBs in your work units. First, employee OCBs are different from employee task performance or on-the-job performance. Second, employee OCBs take many forms, such as working diligently, helping coworkers, and tolerating small inconveniences. Third, work units in which employee OCBs are high are likely to be more productive than work units in which employee OCBs are low. Fourth, there are several ways in which employee OCBs in a work unit contribute to high work unit productivity. Fifth, as a result of these features and contribution of OCBs, it is desirable for a manager to have high levels of employee OCBs in his/her work unit.

The above outlined realizations from your work on Exercise 2 would have helped you to more concretely experience the existence, forms, and desirability of OCBs. Now, Exercise 3 below will further strengthen your experience of some of the specific employee behaviors in various OCB categories and help you to more clearly appreciate the importance of employee OCBs.

Exercise 3: Your best and worst employees and organizational citizenship behavior (OCB)

Directions: *Complete Part A first and Part B next*

Part A: Listed below are a set of statements describing behaviors that an employee might perform at work. Identify the best employee in your work unit (label him/her B) and identify the worst employee in your work unit (label him/her W). Consider a period of about one year. For each statement, indicate the extent to which you agree that the statement describes the identified employee's behavior. Indicate 1 if you 'strongly disagree,' 2 if you 'disagree,' 3 if you 'neither agree nor disagree,' 4 if you 'agree,' and 5 if you 'strongly agree.' The numbers 1 to 5 you need to place in columns with headings "Employee B" and "Employee W" have the meanings as outlined in the following response format.

1	2	3	4	5
Strongly Disagree	Disagree	Neither Agree nor Disagree	Agree	Strongly Agree

Behavior	Employee B	Employee W
1. Tries to do good to the organization.		
2. Works on tasks which are not a part of their job but which may benefit the organization even when they will not receive any rewards in return.		
3. Works even on those organizational tasks that are not likely to get them any rewards.		
4. Promotes cooperation among coworkers without expecting any personal rewards.		
5. Focuses on creating a positive work atmosphere in the organization though it is not a part of their job.		

Note: The above items are partly based on various sources including Borman and Motowidlo (1997), Coleman and Borman (2000), Moorman and Blakely (1995), Organ (1988), Podsakoff et al. (1990), Podsakoff et al. (2000), Smith et al. (1983), and Williams and Anderson (1991), and the descriptions in the preceding parts of this chapter of OCB as employee behaviors in which employees act beyond their formal role requirements, without seeking rewards, for the benefit of the organization (e.g., Organ, 1988). This is a rudimentary set of items prepared only for the purpose of this exercise.

Part B: Compute the overall OCB levels for employees B and W using the following guidelines.

Employee B

After you complete marking responses to the statements in the scale, add the statement scores for employee B as described below.

Statements 1 + 2 + 3 + 4 + 5:____
(Employee B's overall OCB level)

Employee W

After you complete marking responses to the statements in the scale, add the statement scores for employee W as described below.
Statements 1 + 2 + 3 + 4 + 5:____
(Employee W's overall OCB level)

Questions for Reflection: Based on the behaviors listed in the table and the above scores, answer the following questions.

1. How does the best subordinate of yours differ from the worst subordinate of yours? Please describe.
2. Would you prefer all your subordinates to be of type "W" or type "B"?
3. What actions you can take to make sure that all your subordinates are similar to the subordinate type "B"?

Inputs for reflection on Exercise 3: Your answer to the first question above is likely to indicate that your best (B) subordinate has a much higher level of organizational citizenship behaviors than does your worst (W) subordinate. Your answer to the second question above is likely to indicate that you would prefer all your subordinates to perform high levels of organizational citizenship behaviors. This pattern of your answers suggests that it is important for managers that their subordinates perform OCBs. Further, through this exercise you will also see various specific behaviors employees can perform as their OCBs.

This exercise, having helped you to see the importance of employee OCBs, draws your attention to the possible actions you can take to make all your subordinates similar to subordinate "B." While you would have listed some possible actions for enhancing employee OCBs, the topics covered in the subsequent chapters will provide you with several possible actions for enhancing employee OCBs and employees' overall performance. For example, once you understand from the next chapter what employee well-being is and that employee well-being can enhance employee performance, you are likely to be in a position to consider some actions that can help you enhance employee well-being which, in turn, can enhance employee performance. Similarly, as another example, from a subsequent chapter once you understand what organizational justice is and that it can enhance employee OCBs, you are likely to be in a position to consider various actions for enhancing organizational justice in your work unit and thereby to enhance employees' OCBs and organizational performance. Thus, while this chapter has broadened your view of employee performance and helped you realize the importance of employee OCBs and of taking actions for enhancing employee OCBs and overall performance, the subsequent chapters will help you devise various such actions.

Your experience from the previous exercise is likely to help you more concretely see the importance of employee organizational citizenship behaviors or employees' non-task-related positive performance contributions. This realization, based on the previous exercise, will be consistent with the earlier outlined empirical evidence from research indicating that subordinates' contextual performance (a label referring to the behavior category similar to organizational citizenship behaviors) impacts the overall performance ratings assigned by supervisors to subordinates (Borman and Motowidlo, 1997), and that work teams and work units with high OCB levels have high performance (e.g., Podsakoff and MacKenzie, 1997).

The previous parts of this chapter focused on outlining employees' overall performance and the multiple categories of employee behaviors that can be regarded as components of it. It also provided some details on one specific component – OCB – of overall performance. This chapter suggested that employee performance could be viewed as contributions that employees make to facilitate the attainment of goals of an organization. Just as an organization expects employees' performance contributions to facilitate its goal attainment, employees also expect an organization's contribution to enhance their well-being. Thus, the next chapter discusses employee well-being.

References

Borman, W. C. and Motowidlo, S. J. 1997. Task performance and contextual performance: The meaning for personnel selection research. *Human Performance*, 10(2): 99–109.

Coleman, V. I. and Borman, W. C. 2000. Investigating the underlying structure of the citizenship performance domain. *Human Resource Management Review*, 10(1): 25–44.

Eastman, K. K. and Pawar, B. S. 2005. An integrative view of and a common conceptual space for employee extra-role behaviors. In D. L. Turnipseed (Ed.), *Handbook of Organizational Citizenship Behavior: A Review of Good Soldier Activity in Organizations* (pp. 25–46). Nova Science Publishing: Hauppauage, NY.

Fry, L. W. and Slocum, J. W, Jr. 2008. Maximizing the triple bottom line through spiritual leadership. *Organizational Dynamics*, 37(1): 86–96.

Locke, E. A. 1982. The ideas of Frederick W. Taylor: An evaluation. *Academy of Management Review*, 7(1): 14–24.

Moorman, R. H. and Blakely, G. L. 1995. Individualism-collectivism as in individual difference predictor of organizational citizenship behavior. *Journal of Organizational Behavior*, 16: 127–142.

Motowidlo, S. J., Borman, W. C. and Schmit, M. J. 1997. A theory of individual differences in task and contextual performance. *Human Performance*, 10(2): 71–83.

Organ, D. W. 1988. *Organizational Citizenship Behavior: The Good Soldier Syndrome*. Lexington Books: Lexington, MA.

Podsakoff, P. M. and MacKenzie, S. B. 1997. Impact of organizational citizenship behavior on organizational performance: A review and suggestions for future research. *Human Performance*, 10(2): 133–152.

Podsakoff, P. M., MacKenzie, S. B., Moorman, R. H. and Fetter, R. 1990. Transformational leadership behaviors and their effects on followers' trust in leader, satisfaction, organizational citizenship behaviors. *Leadership Quarterly*, 1(2): 107–142.

Podsakoff, P. M., MacKenzie, S. B., Paine, J. B. and Bacharach, D. G. 2000. Organizational citizenship behaviors: A critical review of the theoretical and empirical literature and suggestions for future research. *Journal of Management*, 26: 513–563.

Robinson, S. L. and Bennett, R. J. 1995. A typology of deviant workplace behaviors: A multidimensional scaling study. *Academy of Management Journal*, 38(2): 555–572.

Robinson, S. L. and O'Leary-Kelly, A. M. 1998. Monkey see, monkey do: The influence of work groups on the antisocial behavior of employees. *Academy of Management Journal*, 41(6): 658–672.

Rotundo, M. and Sackett, P. R. 2002. The relative importance of task, citizenship, and counterproductive performance to global ratings of task performance: A policy-capturing approach. *Journal of Applied Psychology*, 87(1): 66–80.

Smith, C. A., Organ, D. W. and Near, J. P. 1983. Organizational citizenship behavior: Its nature and antecedents. *Journal of Applied Psychology*, 68: 653–666.

Taylor, F. W. 1911/2007. *The principles of scientific management*. NuVision Publications: Sioux Falls, SD.

Williams, L. J. and Anderson, S. E. 1991. Job satisfaction and organizational commitment as predictors of organizational citizenship and in-role behaviors. *Journal of Management*, 17: 601–617.

Wren, D. A. 1987. *The Evolution of Management Thought*. John Wiley and Sons: New York, NY.

Chapter 2

Employee well-being

Employees' expectations from an organization

Exercise 1: Your view of employee well-being in a work unit

This exercise is to be completed before reading the chapter. The exercise can facilitate the application of the "well-being" aspect to actual work units.

Directions

Before you read this chapter, do the following exercise for your organization. Using a separate sheet, write down your responses to each of the following questions.

1. Describe your view of what employee well-being means in your own work unit situation.
2. Describe what indicators you would look at to assess the level of employee well-being in your work unit.

After you read the chapter, read your answers to these questions and then reflect on how adequately your responses to the above questions described employee well-being. After reading the chapter, you are likely to realize that your view of well-being, contained in the answers you provided to the above questions before reading this chapter, was somewhat narrow and hence inadequate. You would also realize that this chapter might have helped you develop a more comprehensive view of employee well-being.

Exercise 2: Appreciating employee well-being

Read the descriptions of two organizations below. Based on the descriptions, answer the questions following the description.

Organization A: Employees are competent in doing their tasks. Employee work knowledge and skills are enhanced. Each employee feels that he/she is a good, worthy, and respected individual. Employees can express their individual values in their conduct in the workplace. Employees feel that through their work in the organization, their lives become more meaningful. Employees feel that they have positive relations with others at work. At work, employees experience the emotions of enthusiasm, comfort, calmness, vigor, and pleasure, as opposed to the emotions of boredom, anxiety, anger, fatigue, and depression. Employees feel satisfaction with their overall work. Employees feel that there is trust and mutual support at work. Employees feel that their work is serving society.

Organization B: Employees are not competent in doing their tasks. Employee work knowledge and skills are not enhanced. Each employee feels that he/she is not a good, worthy, or respected individual. Employees cannot express their individual values in their conduct in the workplace. Employees do not feel that through their work in the organization, their lives become more meaningful. Employees feel that they do not have positive relations with others at work. At work, employees experience the emotions of boredom, anxiety, anger, fatigue, and depression, as opposed to the emotions of enthusiasm, comfort, calmness, vigor, and pleasure. Employees do not feel satisfaction with their overall work. Employees feel that there is mistrust and a lack of mutual support at work. Employees feel that their work is not serving society.

1. In which of the above two organizations (A or B) are employees likely to experience a good life?
2. Working in which of the above two organizations is likely to better contribute to employees' quality of life?
3. Which of the above two organizations is more likely to be rated by employees as the best or a great place to work at?
4. In which of the above two organizations is employee performance likely to be higher?

Your responses to these questions are likely to indicate that employees in Organization A are likely to have good life, and that working in Organization A is likely to better contribute to employees' quality of life than is working for Organization B. Your responses are also likely to indicate that Organization A is more likely than Organization B to be rated by employees as a great place to work at.

Finally, your responses are also likely to indicate that employee performance is likely to be higher in Organization A than in Organization B. From this exercise, you may get a general feel that employee well-being refers to positive feelings and functioning and that employee well-being is important, because it contributes to a good quality of life for employees and high employee performance for the organization. These features of well-being realized by you in a general manner through this exercise are described in a more specific and comprehensive manner in the subsequent parts of this chapter.

Employee well-being: What it is?

Human beings require a good life. Well-being is good life and it refers to "optimal experience and functioning" (Ryan and Deci, 2001, p. 141, 142). Employee well-being reflects the quality of positive functioning and positive experiences of employees (Grant, Christianson, and Price, 2007). Thus, for example, when an employee functions competently at work and acquires new work-related skills, he/she is functioning positively. Such positive functioning of an employee is likely to contribute to the enhancement of his/her well-being in the workplace. Further, an employee's experiences of positive feelings (such as enthusiasm or comfort in the workplace) are likely to contribute to the enhancement of his/her well-being at work. Positive functioning can take many forms, such as acquiring skills that fulfill the task requirements or seeking jobs that challenge one's skill levels and thus require one to enhance one's skills. Positive feelings or emotions can also take multiple forms, such as comfort or excitement. As positive functioning and positive emotions take multiple forms, well-being also takes multiple forms.

Employee well-being: Why it is important?

Well-being at work is important for humanitarian reasons. First, employee well-being reflects mental health (e.g., Keyes, 2002). Keyes (2002, p. 208) indicates that "Mental health is, according to the Surgeon General (U.S. Department of Health and Human Services, 1999), … 'a state of successful performance of mental function, resulting in productive activities, fulfilling relationships with people, and the ability to adapt to change and to cope with adversity.'" Keyes (2002, p. 208) links mental health to "subjective well-being," as he notes that "mental health may be operationalized as a syndrome of symptoms of an individual's subjective well-being." He (Keyes, 2002, p. 208) indicates that subjective well-being is "individuals' perceptions and evaluations of their own lives in terms of their affective states and their psychological and social functioning" and operationalizes mental health as "a syndrome of symptoms of positive feelings and positive functioning in life." Keyes (2002, p. 208) notes that the subjective well-being aspects of positive feelings and positive functioning are reflected in different specific forms of well-being. In light of the above outlined link between mental health and well-being, an organization's inadequate provision employee well-being could contribute to the lowering of the mental health of its employees.

Second, the effects of workplace features affect employees' well-being at work, which, in turn, influence employees' well-being in overall life (e.g., Warr, 2005). Thus, inadequate well-being provision by an organization could contribute to lowering employee well-being in overall life. An individual's well-being can positively influence his/her work and income, physical health and life span, and the quality of social relations (Diener and Ryan, 2009, p. 392). In light of such serious consequences of well-being, employee well-being becomes an important aspect for individuals, organizations, and society. Consistent with this, Harter, Schmidt, and Keyes (2002, p. 206) note, "the well-being of employees is in the best interest of communities and organizations." Thus, providing an adequate level of employee well-being in the workplace might be a viewed as an organization's social obligation. The importance of enhancing employee well-being is reflected in the view of Fry and Slocum (2008, p. 86), who note that enhancing employee well-being is "one of the greatest challenges" of the present leaders.

Third, employee well-being is important for utilitarian reasons as well. Employee well-being affects employee performance. This is reflected in the view of Grant et al. (2007, pp. 51–52), who note

> Extensive evidence indicates that employee well-being has a significant impact on the performance and survival of organizations by affecting costs related to illness and health care (Danna and Griffin, 1999), absenteeism, turnover, and discretionary effort (Spector, 1997), organizational citizenship behavior (Podsakoff

et al., 2000), and job performance (Judge, Thoresen, Bono, and Patton, 2001; Wright and Cropanzano, 2000).

Fourth, extracting performance from employees without paying adequate attention to enhancing employee well-being could have adverse consequences. This is reflected in the observations of Gavin and Mason (2004, p. 380), who indicate that while productivity in the US economy has increased, some of the "production-enhancing" practices have had negative implications for employee well-being. Specifically, Gavin and Mason (2004, p. 380) note, "Another pervasive unfavorable outcome of employing these productivity-enhancing practices is a sharp increase in the levels of stress people experience at work. ... The results are disturbing." They (Gavin and Mason, 2004, p. 380) further indicate that

> the effects of stress do not stop at work. They spill out into the rest of workers' lives. In a recent survey of British workers regarding job stress, eight million workers complained that the pressure of work gave them headaches, and 12 million said that they get bad tempered and irritable at home as a result of their workday experiences.

While these views suggest that employee well-being is being impaired because of work and workplace, the issue becomes more serious as employees are putting in extended hours at work (Fry and Cohen, 2009, p. 285). Thus, seeking to enhance employee performance without paying adequate attention to employee well-being can have adverse effects on employees and also on their life outside the workplace.

Thus, it is clear that providing employee well-being is important for an organization for multiple reasons. Providing well-being to employees becomes a significant requirement in light of some indications noted earlier about the present trend of declining employee well-being.

Different forms of well-being

Well-being is the state of positive functioning and positive feelings. The types of positive functioning and the associated positive feelings can span across a wide range. Partly based on various works suggesting different aspects of positive functioning for human

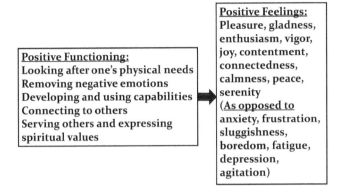

Figure 2.1 Different forms of positive functioning and feeling

Source: Partly based on various works including Diener et al. (1985), Grant et al. (2007), Keyes (1998, 2002), Ryff (1989), and Pawar (2016)

beings (e.g., Diener, Emmons, Larsen, and Griffin, 1985; Grant et al., 2007; Keyes, 1998, 2002; Pawar, 2016; Ryff, 1989), a possible view of this is depicted in Figure 2.1 above.

As well-being requires positive functioning in various areas of one's life and is associated with different shades of positive feelings, well-being takes multiple forms, with each form of well-being reflecting the quality of an individual's functioning and experiences in a different area of life or different facet of human functioning and experiences. Noted in the literature (e.g., Ellison, 1983; Grant et al., 2007; Keyes, 2002) are different forms of well-being: physical, emotional, psychological, social, and spiritual. Each of these forms of well-being is briefly described below.

Physical well-being

Physical well-being refers to the absence of harm to one's physical body, to having good physical health, and to the adequacy of shelter, clothing, food, and mobility (e.g., Grant et al., 2007). At the workplace, this may mean providing employees adequate monetary compensation to enable them to pay for the requirements such as food, clothes, accommodation, and transport. It may also mean providing safe working conditions in the workplace.

Physical well-being in the sense of reasonable monetary compensation and protection from physical injuries in the workplace is likely to be present in quite a few contemporary workplaces. However, there are indications (e.g., Gavin and Mason, 2004) that work stress in increasing. Work stress can have physiological consequences such as increased blood pressure (e.g., Benson, 1974). High blood pressure has been suggested as one cause of severe health problems (Benson, 1974). This suggests that while protection from physical injury is likely to be available in contemporary organizations, work stress could represent another kind of injury to employee health in such organizations.

Emotional well-being

Emotional well-being focuses on the quality of emotions experienced by an individual. Emotions emerge as an outcome of rapid and subconscious appraisal by an individual of an object in terms of its potential for harming or furthering his/her values (e.g., Locke, 1969). Associated with an emotion is an action orientation or tendency to act in a particular way (Locke, 2005). For example, the sight of a destructive explosion or fire may induce the emotion of fear and an action tendency of running away from the spot. Human beings can experience over 100 emotions (Fisher, 2000).

An emotional experience has two dimensions. The first dimension is pleasantness, and emotions along this dimension can range from positive/pleasant to negative/unpleasant feelings (e.g., Warr, 2005). The second component is physiological and involves arousal, which could range from low to high (e.g., Warr, 2005). For example, boredom is an unpleasant/negative emotion with a low arousal level, while anxiety is an unpleasant/negative emotion with a high arousal level (e.g., Warr, 2005, p. 549). Similarly, contentment is a pleasant/positive emotion with a low arousal level, while enthusiasm is a pleasant/positive emotion with a high arousal level (e.g., Warr, 2005, p. 549).

An emotion or emotional experience usually has a short duration and is target specific (e.g., Barsade and Gibson, 2007). Emotions have a short duration in the sense that they emerge and then disappear in a short period. For example, an employee may experience anxiety when his/her machine breaks down, but the anxiety might disappear once the machine is repaired or he/she is assigned to another equally suitable functioning machine to work on. Emotions are also specific to certain objects. For example, an employee may feel anxious about his/her machine's breakdown or may feel bored with his/her current uninteresting task. Possibly because emotions are of a short duration and object specific, it is possible for an individual to experience both positive emotions and negative emotions over a period. For example, at a particular moment, an employee may feel enthusiastic about a new interesting task assigned to him/her and within a few moments if he/she discovers that the raw materials required for completing the task are not available, he/she may feel anxious. Thus, over a period of a day, an employee may experience several positive emotions and several negative emotions.

Emotional well-being, for which affective well-being (e.g., Daniels, 2000) is another term, reflects a hedonic or pleasure-oriented form of well-being. The hedonic form of well-being refers to the experience of a high level of positive emotions and a low level of negative emotions (e.g., Ryan and Deci, 2001). Positive emotions include enthusiasm, excitement, joy, calmness, tranquility, etc. Negative emotions include boredom, depression, anxiety, anger, etc. Thus, if an employee frequently experiences several negative emotions and relatively less frequently experiences only a few positive emotions, then his/her emotional well-being will be at a low level.

Related to emotional well-being is another related well-being form referred to as subjective well-being. Presence of positive mood, absence of negative mood, and satisfaction with life form the constituents of subjective well-being (Ryan and Deci, 2001, p. 144). Similarly, Diener et al. (1985, p. 71) note that positive affect, negative affect, and life satisfaction are components of subjective well-being. One way of deriving subjective well-being level from these components is to add the level of satisfaction with life to the level of positive affect and then subtract the level of negative affect from it (e.g., Page and Vella-Brodrick, 2013, p. 1012).

Psychological well-being

Psychological well-being refers to positive functioning. Psychological well-being focuses on whether an individual is functioning in a manner to realize the human potential or one's true potential. Ryan and Deci (2001, p. 146) characterize psychological well-being by noting "Ryff and Singer (1998, 2000) ... drawing on Aristotle, they describe well-being not simply as the attaining of pleasure, but as 'the striving for perfection that represents the realization of one's true potential' (Ryff, 1995, p. 100)." A view in the literature (e.g., Ryan and Deci, 2001; Ryff, 1989) is that psychological well-being reflects a good life and it emerges from seeking perfection and from fulfilling one's true or objective needs embedded in the real nature of human beings rather than pursuing the fulfillment of one's subjective desires. In this view, pursuit of desires is suggested to have potential for negative consequences, and living to attain or express one's true nature or objective needs is suggested to be a good life and psychological well-being. Thus, this view suggests psychological well-being as coming from potential-fulfilling rather than from pleasure-seeking through the pursuit of one's subjectively felt desires. This distinction indicates the difference between subjective happiness or emotional well-being and psychological well-being.

The state of having psychological well-being is characterized by the positive experiences of having high self-acceptance, being able to master the environment, experiencing growth in terms of making considerable use of one's capabilities, having autonomy (internal evaluation norms), having a sense of direction or life purpose, and having good interpersonal relations (Keyes, Shmotkin, and Ryff, 2002, p. 1008; Ryan and Deci, 2001, p. 146; Ryff, 1989, p. 1071). These aspects are elaborated further below based on Keyes et al. (2002, p. 1008), Ryan and Deci (2001, p. 146), Ryff (1989, p. 1071–1072), and the operationalization of psychological well-being in the "Mental Health Continuum – Short Form" (MHC-SF) (Keyes, 2009) and "Mental Health Continuum – Long Form" (MHC-LF) (Keyes, 2002). Self-acceptance involves feelings of being satisfied with one's overall life and liking oneself as an individual. Being able to master the environment reflects feelings of being able to manage the demands of one's daily life. In the work context, this might mean managing well one's work and work relations. Personal growth involves developing capabilities. Autonomy is reflected in having confidence in one's opinions and assessing oneself in terms of one's own belief about what is important. A sense of life purpose means having an aim for one's future life. Having good interpersonal relations refers to having close relationships with others.

Social well-being

Social well-being refers to "the appraisal of one's circumstance and functioning in the society" (Keyes, 1998, p. 122). Thus, high social well-being is likely to be reflected in one's positive assessment of the conditions and circumstances of one's social life. Social well-being is reflected in the experiences of social integration, social contribution, social coherence, social acceptance, and social actualization (Keyes, 1998, pp. 122–123). Social integration refers to the extent to which an individual feels that he/she belongs to a community or society and has commonalities with other individuals in the society (Keyes, 1998, pp. 122–123; Keyes, 2002, p. 209, 212). Social contribution focuses on the feelings of the extent to which one makes a positive or valuable contribution to the society and thereby forms a significant part of the society (Keyes, 1998, p. 123). Social coherence reflects the feeling that one can make sense out of and predict how the society functions (Keyes, 1998, p. 123). This feeling focuses on being able to understand and see the order in the social system. Social acceptance focuses on having a belief that people in the society are in general good in terms of kindness and capability and hence can be trusted (Keyes, 1998, p. 122). Social actualization involves the feeling that the society is evolving positively (Keyes, 1998, p. 123).

Based on the above description of various aspects of social well-being, an individual with high social well-being is likely to feel that he/she belongs to and is an important and contributing part of a society that is evolving positively, which he/she understands, and in which people in general are kind and can be trusted. This form of well-being seems to reflect the extent to which one's social life provides a sense of relatedness, significance, predictability, acceptability, and hope. Thus, employees' social well-being in the workplace is likely to be reflected in such feelings and experiences as feelings of belongingness to the organization, belief that the organization is improving, feeling that one understands how the organization functions, and feeling that coworkers are kind and trustworthy.

Spiritual well-being

While a brief integrative view of spiritual well-being is outlined in Pawar (2016), a more elaborate identification of various aspects of spiritual well-being is described below. Spiritual well-being focuses on the extent to which one's spiritual needs are fulfilled or the quality of the spiritual side of one's life (e.g., Ellison, 1983). The spiritual aspect refers to something in contrast with the material or physical (e.g., Moberg and Brusek, 1978, pp. 313–314) or to the non-physical (e.g., Ellison, 1983) aspect. It refers to the fulfillment of the need for transcendence (Ellison, 1983). The link between the need for transcendence and spirituality is reflected in the view of Paloutzian, Emmons, and Keortge (2003, p. 124) that "This need for transcendence expresses itself as what is commonly called 'spirituality.'"

The term 'transcendence' refers to going beyond oneself, or stepping back from or climbing up to (Ellison, 1983; Mirvis, 1997). Thus, spiritual fulfillment or fulfillment of the need for transcendence can be reflected in going beyond oneself or one's material and physical self. Since an individual's concern for his/her own self is likely to be expressed through his/her concern for self-interests, spiritual fulfillment or fulfillment of the need for transcendence can be seen as transcendence of self-interests. The relationship between transcendence and spirituality is reflected in the view of Ellison (1983, pp. 331–332, emphasis original) who notes, "It is the *spirit* of human beings which enables and motivates us to search for meaning and purpose in life, to seek the supernatural or some meaning which transcends us, to wonder about our origins and our identities, to require morality and equity." This view indicates that the spirit motivates an individual to search for the supernatural or meaning that transcends him/her and implies that spirituality is reflected in the transcendence.

The relationship between transcendence, purpose, spirituality, and spiritual well-being is reflected in the view of Paloutzian et al. (2003, p. 124), who noted,

> I get a sense of spiritual fulfilment from it, a sense of well-being that comes no other way. This reflects a need for transcendence, a need for purpose, and a built-in tendency toward spirituality that is part of what makes a person human.

The above view also suggests that spirituality is reflected in seeking meaning or purpose which transcends oneself. This link between spirituality and meaning or purpose is also implied by Paloutzian et al. (2003, p. 125), who note that "Nonreligious spirituality, whether or not a person justifies in an ultimate philosophical sense, is the striving for the fulfilment of any value, goal, or higher calling that the individual believes to be meaningful."

The nature of experiences in spiritual well-being can be understood by considering some of the items in the scales that seek to measure spiritual well-being. Paloutzian and Ellison (1982) developed a measure of spiritual well-being consisting of the two dimensions of existential well-being and religious well-being mentioned in the earlier pioneering work of Moberg and Brusek (1978, p. 231). The existential well-being dimension has items reflecting satisfaction with life and having a sense of purpose, meaning, and direction, while religious well-being dimension has items reflecting the quality of one's relationship with God. The items in Paloutzian and Ellison's (1982) measure indicate that existential well-being refers to feelings such as having meaning, direction, purpose, order in life, and life satisfaction, which may possibly reflect fulfillment of purpose or attainment of a sense of meaning. The items in Paloutzian and Ellison's (1982) measure of religious well-being refer to feelings such as having a connection with God, receiving love of God, and receiving support from God. The dimensions in the other measure of spiritual well-being in Moberg (1984) included Christian faith, satisfaction with self, personal piety, and subjective spiritual well-being. The Christian faith dimension includes items that reflect faith in God, relationship with God, and receiving meaning and help from one's faith. The self-satisfaction dimension includes items that reflect feelings of happiness, meaning, and purpose in life and having inner peace and harmony. The personal piety dimension includes items reflecting engagement in activities such as reading devotional literature, engaging in meditation, and performing private prayers. The above descriptions of two scales measuring spiritual well-being suggest that spiritual well-being is the extent of engagement in the activities that seek God, existence of faith in or relationship with God, and experiences of peace, harmony, happiness, meaning, and purpose in life.

The above description of spiritual well-being suggests that employees' spiritual well-being at work is likely to be reflected in feeling that one can engage in activities at work that allow one to connect to God and to experience meaning, purpose, peace, and harmony. Both of the above examples of measuring spiritual well-being have a focus on faith or God and on positive experiences and feelings such as peace in life. While acknowledging and seeking to establish a relationship with God is one way of seeking transcendence, another way could be to go beyond oneself or one's self-interests by serving others, by making positive contributions to society, and by establishing relationships with others in which one fulfills one's obligations as a community member. This latter view of self-transcendence is reflected in the definition of spirituality by Benson, Roehlkepartain, and Rude (2003). Self-transcendence or spirituality can also come from expressing higher values such as mercy, kindness, compassion, and caring. This is consistent with a view of spirituality as involving higher values (Fairholm, 1997, cited in Fry, 2003, p. 702), reference to values such as fairness, humility, and honesty (Reave, 2005) as spiritual values, and inclusion of the values such as forgiveness, compassion, and gratitude as a part of spiritual intelligence (e.g., Paloutzian et al., 2003, pp. 127–128).

Based on the various descriptions of spirituality and spiritual well-being noted above, spiritual well-being reflects an individual's experience of going beyond themselves in experiencing peace and a connection with God, in serving others through their work (meaning and higher purpose), in establishing contribution-providing relationship with others, and in expressing spiritual values. A similar view is provided in Pawar (2016). Thus, an employee experiencing high spiritual well-being is likely to have the experiences of having some relationship with God, serving the society through work (e.g., having meaning and higher purpose), having a contribution-providing relationship with coworkers, having peace, and expressing spiritual values at work (e.g., Pawar, 2016).

The multiple forms of employee well-being described above are depicted in an integrated form in Figure 2.2.

In the preceding part, five forms of employee well-being – physical, emotional, psychological, social, and spiritual – are described. The descriptions of these five forms of well-being indicate the differences between them. For example, as outlined above, emotional well-being focuses on having more positive than negative feelings, while psychological well-being focuses on functioning involving experiences such as competence, autonomy, and purpose. Similarly, spiritual well-being focuses on functioning involving the expression of interpersonal spiritual values such as kindness and the resulting feelings such as peace. Such fine differences distinguish multiple forms of well-being. However, all these well-being forms can contribute to and constitute parts of an individual's overall well-being. Further, there could be relationships between various forms of well-being. For example, Pawar (2016) reported empirical evidence on positive correlations between emotional, psychological, social, and spiritual well-being. Similarly, Keyes (2005) reported empirical evidence on positive correlations between emotional, psychological, and social well-being. Thus, while different forms of well-being have distinct features, they are also related, to some extent, to each other and all constitute parts of overall well-being. Some of the differences between different forms of well-being and their interrelationships will also be clear through the work on the exercises included at the end of this chapter.

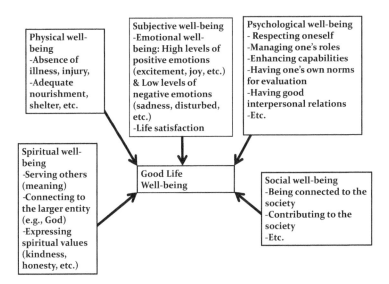

Figure 2.2 An integrated overview of multiple forms of well-being

Source: Physical well-being is partly based on Grant et al. (2007); psychological well-being is partly based on Keyes (2002), Ryan and Deci (2001), and Ryff (1989, p. 1071–1072); social well-being is partly based on Keyes (1998, p. 122–123; 2002, p. 209, 212); subjective well-being is partly based on Diener et al. (1985, p. 71–72) and Ryan and Deci (2001, p. 144); emotional well-being is partly based on Daniels (2000); and spiritual well-being is partly based on Pawar (2016)

Well-being is not absence of mental ill-health but presence of positive mental health

Well-being is good life in terms of positive functioning and positive feeling. In the view of Keyes (2002, p. 208), positive functioning and positive feeling is characterized by "mental health." Thus, well-being, in the view of Keyes (2002, p. 210), is mental health. Keyes (2002, p. 210) indicates that the presence of complete mental health indicates flourishing, and the presence of incomplete mental health (positive functioning and feeling) indicates languishing (which Keyes [2002, p. 213] also refers to as absence of mental health), while the levels between these two reflect moderate mental health or well-being or "*moderately mentally healthy*" individuals (emphasis original).

The above discussion suggests that mental ill-health is not merely the absence of positive functioning and feeling, but it is the presence of negative functioning and negative feelings such as depression. A person who does not have mental ill-health may have moderate levels of mental health or well-being characterized by moderate levels of positive functioning and feelings. He/she, however, will not necessarily have complete well-being, which is characterized by high levels of positive functioning such as being competent and expressing one's values.

Well-being is not absence of work stress

Absence of work stress for employees does not necessarily suggest that employees have high well-being. This is because of three aspects. First, in terms of emotions, the experience of work stress is characterized by negative emotions such as anxiety and frustration. Second, such negative emotions are a subset of their part in affective or emotional well-being (e.g., Daniels, 2000). Third, one of the five categories of well-being covered above is subjective well-being, which is characterized by high levels of positive emotions, low levels of negative emotions, and job satisfaction. Therefore, the negative emotions associated with work stress experienced are only a subset of the negative emotions component of subjective well-being.

Thus, absence of employee work stress, by itself, can suggest that the negative emotions part of subjective well-being is likely to be low, and hence it is likely to contribute to high levels of employees' subjective well-being. However, absence of employee work stress, by itself, does not indicate whether other forms of employee well-being, such as spiritual well-being and psychological well-being, will be high.

Enhancing employee well-being requires going beyond removing stress and mental ill-health

From the above description, it should be clear that for enhancing employee well-being, it is not sufficient to take actions to reduce employees' work stress or to avoid mental ill-health. This is so because, as the preceding discussion indicates, absence of work stress may only contribute to the lowering of negative emotions and hence to an increase in employees' emotional well-being. The other forms of employee well-being are not likely to be necessarily enhanced through reduction in negative emotions coming from the absence of work stress. Similarly, the above discussion based on Keyes (2002) suggests that avoiding mental ill-health may not provide the state of complete well-being or flourishing

Well-being in life and at work

In the preceding parts, physical, emotional, psychological, social, and spiritual well-being forms were discussed with an implicit focus on the overall life context of an individual. However, just as an individual's well-being can be assessed in the overall life context, it can also be assessed in the specific context of work (e.g., Warr, 2005). For example, emotional well-being at work could be reflected in having more positive than negative emotions emerging from work-related features and events. Similarly, employees' psychological well-being at work could be reflected in the experiences of being competent at one's work, developing one's talents and capabilities at work, feeling good about oneself in terms of one's functioning in the workplace, being able to use one's own standards and not being unduly influenced by others' opinions in making one's decisions at work, having a sense of purpose and direction to one's career path at work, and having positive relations with others at work. Social well-being in the work context could be reflected in the experiences of feeling a sense of belonging to the workplace social system, contributing to and being a significant part of the workplace social system, understanding how the workplace social system operates, feeling that the workplace social system has a positive potential, and feeling that the members of workplace social system are in general good, kind, capable, and trustworthy. It might be difficult to distinguish spiritual well-being in the overall life context from spiritual well-being at work because of the nature of experiences associated with spiritual well-being, which include faith in God, receiving meaning and help from faith in God, expressing higher values, and experiencing peace, harmony, and happiness. Possibly, spiritual well-being in the work context could be reflected in the experiences of being able to uphold or practice at work one's faith in God, receiving meaning and help at work through one's faith in God, being able to express higher values at work, and the work's contribution to one's experiencing peace, harmony, and happiness at work.

This and the preceding chapter described employee performance, which is an organization's requirement from employees, and employee well-being, which is employees' requirement from an organization. The next chapter describes how employee performance and employee well-being are two desired outcomes for an organization. Chapters after the next focus on various organizational actions or features that can enhance employee performance and well-being. Thus, the Chapter 4 describes some of the traditional approaches to enhancing employee performance and wellbeing, and the chapters following that cover the organizational features of transformational leadership, organizational justice, organizational support, and workplace spirituality. After these chapters, some inputs are provided on how these organizational features can be implemented for enhancing employee performance and well-being.

Reflection on Exercise 1: Your view of employee well-being in a work unit

In Exercise 1, you would have described, based on your understanding before reading this chapter, employee well-being and its possible indicators. Now, read your description and, in light of your present understanding based on the reading of this chapter, assess how adequate your understanding, reflected in the description you provided in Exercise 1, of employee well-being was before reading the chapter. You are likely to realize that your understanding of employee well-being and its indicators before reading this chapter was narrow and inadequate. From this realization, you would appreciate the value of this chapter for enhancing your understanding of employee well-being.

Exercise 3: Assessing well-being in overall life

Consider the description of various components of well-being – physical, emotional, psychological, social, and spiritual well-being – outlined in the earlier parts of this chapter. Based on the type of feelings and functioning that are associated with each of these wellbeing forms, make a thoughtful judgment of the level at which you experience various well-being forms in your overall life. Based on your judgment, indicate your assessment of:

1. What is the level of your overall well-being in life? (High, moderate, or low)
2. What is the level of your physical well-being in life? (High, moderate, or low)
3. What is the level of your emotional well-being in life? (High, moderate, or low)
4. What is the level of your psychological well-being in life? (High, moderate, or low)
5. What is the level of your social well-being in life? (High, moderate, or low)
6. What is the level of your spiritual well-being in life? (High, moderate, or low)

Based on the above assessments of your well-being level in your overall life, made by you, respond to the following statements.

1. Describe whether your overall level of well-being is low, moderate, or high.
2. Describe how you feel about your overall well-being level.
3. Describe how your overall well-being affects your work in your organization.
4. Describe how your overall well-being affects you as a person.
5. Describe how you can enhance your level of overall well-being.
6. Indicate the likely overall well-being level for most of the employees in your work unit or organization.
7. What is the overall well-being level – high, moderate, or low – you would like employees in your organization to have?
8. Describe what actions you can take to enhance the overall well-being for most of the employees in your work unit or organization.

Reflection on Exercise 3: Assessing well-being (in overall life)

Consider your responses to questions 2, 3, and 4. From these responses you may see that depending on whether your well-being level is high, moderate, or low, you are likely to experience respectively very positive, somewhat positive, or negative consequences for your work and also for your functioning and feeling as a person.

From your assessment of your well-being level and its consequences for your work and for you as a person, you may realize that it is desirable to provide a high level of well-being for employees in your work unit and organization.

Your responses to questions 5 and 8 are likely to contain a few actions for enhancing your own well-being and that of employees in your work unit or organization. Examine how adequately the actions identified by you reflect the understanding of positive functioning and feeling associated with various well-being forms described in the earlier parts of this chapter. If you have been able to identify very few actions for enhancing well-being in response to questions 5 and 8, then you may again read the descriptions of various well-being forms in the earlier parts of this chapter and then, based on these descriptions, identify some more actions for enhancing well-being. After reading the subsequent chapters on transformational leadership, organizational justice, organizational support, and workplace spirituality and after reaching the end of the book, you may be able to identify many more specific actions for enhancing employee well-being.

Exercise 4: Assessing work well-being

Exercise 3 was intended to help you assess your own overall well-being in life and, by extension, that of your employees. Research (e.g., Warr, 2005) indicates that well-being in the work context is different from well-being in overall life. This is similar to the difference that exists between job satisfaction and life satisfaction. Now, Exercise 4 should help you assess your, and by extension your subordinates', well-being in the specific domain of work.

Questions to answer and reflections on answers

Consider the description of various components of well-being – physical, emotional, psychological, social, and spiritual well-being – outlined in the earlier parts of this chapter. Based on the type of feelings and functioning that are associated with each of these well-being forms, make a thoughtful judgment of the level at which you experience various well-being forms in your workplace. Based on your judgment, indicate your assessment of:

1. What is the level of your overall well-being in your workplace? (High, moderate, or low)
2. What is the level of your physical well-being in your workplace? (High, moderate, or low)
3. What is the level of your emotional well-being in your workplace? (High, moderate, or low)
4. What is the level of your psychological well-being in your workplace? (High, moderate, or low)
5. What is the level of your social well-being in your workplace? (High, moderate, or low)
6. What is the level of your spiritual well-being your workplace? (High, moderate, or low)

Based on the above assessments, of your well-being level in your workplace, made by you, respond to the following statements.

1. Describe whether your work well-being is low, moderate, or high.
2. Describe how you feel about your work well-being level.
3. Describe how the level of your work well-being level affects your work in your organization.
4. Describe how your work well-being level affects you as a person.
5. Describe how you can enhance your level of work well-being.
6. Indicate the likely work well-being level for most of the employees in your work unit or organization.
7. What is the work well-being level – high, moderate, or low – that you would like employees in your organization to have?
8. Describe what actions you can take to enhance the work well-being level for most of the employees in your work unit or organization.

Reflection on Exercise 4: Assessing work well-being (job-related well-being in workplace)

Consider your responses to questions 2, 3, and 4. From these responses you may see that depending on whether your work well-being level is high, moderate, or low, you are likely to experience respectively very positive, somewhat positive, or negative consequences for your work and also for your functioning and feeling as a person. From your assessment of your work well-being and its consequences for your work and for you as a person, you may realize that it is desirable to provide a high level of work well-being for employees in your work unit and organization.

Your responses to questions 5 and 8 are likely to contain a few actions for enhancing your own work well-being and that of employees in your work unit or organization. Examine how adequately the actions identified by you reflect the understanding of positive functioning and feeling associated with various well-being forms described in the earlier parts of this chapter. If you have been able to identify very few actions for enhancing work well-being in response to questions 5 and 8, then you may again read the descriptions of various well-being forms in the earlier parts of this chapter and then, based on these descriptions, identify some more actions for enhancing work well-being. After reading the subsequent chapters on transformational leadership, organizational justice, organizational support, and workplace spirituality and after reaching the end of the book, you may be able to identify many more specific actions for enhancing employee work well-being.

Some learning points from exercises

Now if you read your responses to Exercise 1 at the beginning of the chapter, you would realize that your view of employee well-being was probably narrower than the view described in the chapter. If you read your responses in Exercise 2, you would realize that while you may have had a general idea that employee well-being is important, the chapter contents provide a much more precise understanding of the wide-ranging positive consequences and, therefore, importance of employee well-being. Thus, the two chapter-opening exercises are beneficial in understanding employee well-being.

If you read your responses to questions 5 and 8 of the end-of-the-chapter Exercise 3 and Exercise 4, you would see that you have probably identified only a few actions for enhancing employee well-being. After you complete reading the remaining parts of the book, you may see that you can identify many more actions for enhancing employee well-being than you did at the end of this chapter.

References

Barsade, S. G. and Gibson, D. E. 2007. Why does affect matter in organizations? *Academy of Management Perspectives*, February: 36–59.

Benson, H. 1974. Your innate asset for combating stress. *Harvard Business Review*, July–August: 49–60.

Benson, P. L., Roehlkepartain, E. L. and Rude, S. P. 2003. Spiritual development in childhood and adolescence: Toward a field of inquiry. *Applied Developmental Science*, 7(3): 205–213.

Danna, K. and Griffin, R. W. 1999. Health and well-being in the workplace: A review and synthesis of the literature. *Journal of Management*, 25(3): 357–384.

Daniels, K. 2000. Measures of five aspects of affective well-being at work. *Human Relations*, 53(2): 275–294.

Diener, E., Emmons, R. A., Larsen, R. J. and Griffin, S. 1985. The satisfaction with life scale. *Journal of Personality Assessment*, 41(1): 71–75.

Diener, E. and Ryan, K. 2009. Subjective well-being: A general overview. *South African Journal of Psychology*, 39(4): 391–406.

Ellison, C. W. 1983. Spiritual well-being: Conceptualization and measurement. *Journal of Psychology and Theology*, 11(4): 330–340.

Fisher, C. D. 2000. Mood and emotions while working: Missing pieces of job satisfaction? *Journal of Organizational Behavior*, 21: 185–202.

Fry, L. W. 2003. Toward a theory of spiritual leadership. *Leadership Quarterly*, 24: 693–727.

Fry, L. W. and Cohen, M. P. 2009. Spiritual leadership as a paradigm for organizational transformation and recovery from extended work hours culture. *Journal of Business Ethics*, 84: 265–278.

Fry, L. W. and Slocum, J. W, Jr. 2008. Maximizing the triple bottom line through spiritual leadership. *Organizational Dynamics*, 37(1): 86–96.

Gavin, H. G. and Mason, R. O. 2004. The virtuous organization: The value of happiness in the workplace. *Organizational Dynamics*, 33(4): 379–392.

Grant, A. M., Christianson, M. K. and Price, R. H. 2007. Happiness, health, or relationships? Managerial practices and employee well-being tradeoffs. *Academy of Management Perspectives*, 21(3): 51–63.

Harter, J. K., Schmidt, F. L. and Keyes, C. L. M. 2002. Well-being in the workplace and its relationship to business outcomes: A review of the Gallup studies. In C. L. M. Keyes and J. Haidt (Eds.), *Flourishing: The Positive Person and the Good Life* (pp. 205–224). American Psychological Association: Washington, DC.

Judge, T. A., Thoresen, C. J., Bono, J. E. and Patton, G. K. 2001. The job satisfaction-job performance relationship: A qualitative and quantitative review. *Psychological Bulletin*, 127: 376–407.

Keyes, C. L. M. 1998. Social well-being. *Social Psychology Quarterly*, 61(2): 121–140.

Keyes, C. L. M. 2002. The mental health continuum: From languishing to flourishing in life. *Journal of Health and Social Research*, 43, June: 207–222.

Keyes, C. L. M. 2005. Mental illness and/or mental health? Investigating axioms of the complete state model of health. *Journal of Consulting and Clinical Psychology*, 73(3): 539–548.

Keyes, C. L. M. 2009. *Brief Description of the Mental Health Continuum Short Form (MHC-SF)*. Atlanta.

Keyes, C. L. M., Shmotkin, D. and Ryff, C. D. 2002. Optimizing well-being: The empirical encounter of two traditions. *Journal of Personality and Social Psychology*, 82: 1007–1022.

Locke, E. A. 1969. What is job satisfaction? *Organizational Behavior and Human Performance*, 4: 309–336.

Locke, E. A. 2005. Why emotional intelligence is an invalid concept? *Journal of Organizational Behavior*, 26: 425–431.

Mirvis, P. H. 1997. Soul work' in Organizations. *Organization Science*, 8(2): 190–206.

Moberg, D. O. 1984. Measures of spiritual well-being. *Review of Religious Research*, 25(4): 351–364.

Moberg, D. O. and Brusek, P. J. 1978. Spiritual well-being: A neglected subject in quality of life research. *Social Indicators Research*, 5(3): 303–323.

Page, K. M. and Vella-Brodrick, D. A. 2013. The working for a wellness program: RCT of an employee well-being intervention. *Journal of Happiness Studies*, 14: 1007–1031.

Paloutzian, R. F. and Ellison, C. W. 1982. Loneliness, spiritual well-being and the quality of life. In L. A. Peplau and D. Perlman (Eds.), *Loneliness: A Sourcebook of Current Theory, Research, and Therapy* (pp. 224–237). Wiley Interscience: New York, NY.

Paloutzian, R. F., Emmons, R. A. and Keortge, S. G. 2003. Spiritual well-being, spiritual intelligence, and healthy workplace policy. In R. A. Giacalone and C. L. Jurkiewicz (Eds.), *The Handbook of Workplace Spirituality and Organizational Performance* (pp. 123–136). ME. Sharpe: Armonk, NY.

Pawar, B. S. 2016. Workplace spirituality and employee well-being: An empirical examination. *Employee Relations: The International Journal*, 38(6): 975–994.

Reave, L. 2005. Spiritual values and practices related to leadership effectiveness. *Leadership Quarterly*, 16: 655–687.

Ryan, R. M. and Deci, E. L. 2001. On happiness and human potentials: A review of research on hedonic and eudaimonic well-being. *Annual Review of Psychology*, 52: 141–166.

Ryff, C. D. 1989. Happiness is everything, or is it? Exploration on the meaning of psychological well-being. *Journal of Personality and Social Psychology*, 57: 1069–1081.

Warr, P. 2005. Work, well-being, and mental health. In J. Barling, E. K. Kelloway and M. R. Frone (Eds.), *Handbook of Work Stress* (pp. 547–573). Sage: Thousand Oaks, CA.

Chapter 3

Employee performance and employee well-being

Two desired outcomes for an organization

Linkages between employee performance and employee well-being

The preceding two chapters focused on employee performance and employee well-being respectively. There are some linkages between employee performance and employee well-being. First, as outlined in the following section, an organization needs to attain both employee performance and employee well-being in order for it to be a healthy organization in the long term. Second, as noted in the subsequent parts of this chapter, there is empirical evidence indicating that employee well-being is positively associated with employee performance, which suggests that employee well-being influences employee performance. Third, the chapter also indicates that in the process of attaining one of these two outcomes, an organization might focus on one and possibly undermine the other. Such linkages between employee performance and employee well-being are outlined in the course of the chapter. It also points out that the main action areas – leadership, justice, support, and workplace spirituality – covered in the subsequent chapters of this book can help in enhancing both employee performance and well-being.

The need for an organization to focus on both employee performance and employee well-being

Employee performance is an important outcome to seek for an organization. Employee performance is a judgment of the extent to which an employee's behaviors facilitate organizational goal attainment (Borman and Motowidlo, 1997). Hence, employee performance is a determinant of organizational goal attainment. Employee performance is regarded as one of the two critical objectives sought by a healthy organization (e.g., Wilson, DeJoy, Vandenberg, Richardson, and McGrath, 2004).

Employee well-being is another important outcome to seek for an organization. Specifically, the definition of a healthy organization provided by Wilson et al. (2004, p. 567) notes, "A healthy organization is one characterized by intentional, systematic, and collaborative efforts to maximize employee well-being and productivity by providing well-designed and meaningful jobs, a supportive social-organizational environment, and accessible and equitable opportunities for career and work-life enhancement." This definition suggests that maximized employee well-being is one of the outcomes characterizing a healthy organization. Further, employee well-being can also affect the second outcome feature – employee productivity – of a healthy organization. The influence of employee well-being on employee productivity is reflected in the assessment of Grant, Christianson, and Price (2007, pp. 51–52), that

> Extensive evidence indicates that employee well-being has a significant impact on the performance and survival of organizations by affecting costs related to illness and health care (Danna and Griffin, 1999), absenteeism, turnover, and discretionary effort (Spector, 1997), organizational citizenship behaviour (Podsakoff et al., 2000), and job performance (Judge et al., 2001; Wright and Cropanzano, 2000).

Thus, employee well-being is a feature of healthy work organizations, and it also affects employee productivity, which is another feature of a healthy organization. The above discussion indicates that employee well-being is important for organizational health. Consistent with this, Harter, Schmidt, and Keyes (2002, p. 206) note, "The well-being of employees is in the best interest of communities and organizations."

The preceding discussion indicates the significance of employee well-being for organizational health (e.g., Wilson et al., 2004) and for organizations (e.g., Grant et al., 2007; Harter et al., 2002). However, Gavin and Mason (2004, p. 380) have expressed concerns about the recent decline in employee well-being in some contexts. This further enhances the criticality of employee well-being for organizations.

Given the significance of employee well-being and performance for organizational health, focusing on both is important for organizations. Consistent with this, Fry and Slocum (2008, p. 86) note, "one of the greatest challenges facing leaders today is the need to develop new business models that accentuate ethical leadership, employee well-being, sustainability, and social responsibility without sacrificing profitability, revenue growth, and other indicators of financial performance." In this assessment of Fry and Slocum (2008, p. 86), the "profitability, revenue growth, and other indicators of financial performance" aspects are likely to be reflections of employee performance. Thus, the above assessment of Fry and Slocum (2008, p. 86) suggests that enhancing employee well-being and employee performance is one of the "greatest challenges" of contemporary leaders.

Challenges in attaining employee performance and well-being

While employee performance and well-being are two desired outcomes for an organization, there are likely to be certain challenges in an organization's attaining them. Some of such likely challenges are outlined below.

One challenge in enhancing employee performance and well-being is that there is a possibility of focusing more on either employee performance or employee well-being. This possibility is reflected in the two situations from the literature outlined below.

Consider the example of public sector banks in India. In 1969, some of the private sector banks were nationalized, and their status was changed from private sector banks to public sector banks. During the period from about 1969 to about 1990, employee welfare received considerable attention possibly because of trade unions' attempts to protect beneficial work conditions for employees. This focus of employee trade unions is reflected in the observation in The Report of the Committee on the Financial System, "While trade unions have performed their legitimate function of looking after service conditions of their members ..." (Narasimham, 1991, p. 35). During those periods, the efficiency of banks was less than satisfactory, as noted in an observation in The Report of the Committee on the Financial System that "productivity and efficiency of the system have suffered" (Narasimham, 1991, p. 3). As an organization's efficiency is partly influenced by employee performance, the simultaneous occurrence of employee welfare and low organizational efficiency, in the above example, suggests that the focus on employee well-being undermined employee performance. This possibility is reflected in another observation, which notes,

> A situation has arisen today where emoluments of the bank staff and their revisions are no longer directly related to either productivity or profitability of either individual banks or of the system. This has aggravated the situation of some of the weaker constituents of the system. Studies undertaken by the Reserve Bank indicate that labour productivity (measured either in terms of per capita net income or in terms of cost of different activities per rupee of established costs) has been declining. The rate of growth in staff costs has been higher than that of the surplus in banks.
>
> (Narasimham, 1991, p. 36)

The Report of the Committee on the Financial System (Narasimham, 1991, pp. 35–36) points out actions or policies such as overstaffing, accelerated promotions, salary increases, restrictive work practices including work norms, staff transfer constraints, and resistance to technology upgrades. Some of these actions or policies seem to have been influenced by employee trade unions and may have been aimed at enhancing employee well-being. Increased labor costs from policies of overstaffing along with salary increases, without commensurate gains in employee performance, may have been one of the possible reasons for the lower productivity or profitability of banks.

In contrast to the above situation, it is likely that focus on employee performance may undermine employee well-being. Gavin and Mason (2004, p. 380) note,

> Since the U.S. economy took off during the early 1970s, national productivity has increased sharply. Whereas the national average annual productivity gain from 1970 to 2003 was 2.3%, from 1995 to 2003 productivity increases surged to a rate of 3.2% per annum.

Gavin and Mason (2004, p. 380) further note that the adoption of productivity-improving practices dehumanizes employees' jobs and that "another pervasive unfavourable outcome of employing these productivity-enhancing practices is a sharp increase in the levels of stress people experience at work ... the results are disturbing." Gavin and Mason (2004, pp. 380–381) present data indicating an increase in stress level and drop in satisfaction with job of American workers. Another expression of Gavin and Mason (2004, p. 390) suggests the occurrence of employee performance while undermining employee well-being, as they note, "In recent years economic productivity has been wrung out of the average employee, in large measure, at the cost of his or her health and happiness." The above two examples suggest that focusing more on either employee performance or employee well-being might result in facilitating employee well-being while impairing performance or improving performance while undermining employee well-being.

Another challenge is in enhancing employee well-being alone. As employee well-being has multiple forms, enhancing one form of employee well-being can impair another form of employee well-being. Grant et al. (2007, p. 54) draw upon research to illustrate how four managerial practices – job redesign, incentive provision, team-building, and safety enhancement – can cause an increase in some form of employee well-being while lowering another form of employee well-being. For example, Grant et al. (2007, p. 54) note, "research indicates that work redesign practices can increase psychological well-being but decrease physical well-being, providing clear evidence of well-being tradeoffs."

Feasibility of enhancing employee performance and well-being

While there is a challenge in simultaneously enhancing both employee performance and well-being, it is feasible to do so. For example, the outcomes of organizational justice include both employee performance and some forms of employee well-being (Cohen-Charash and Spector, 2001). This implies that providing a greater amount of organizational justice can enhance both employee performance and some forms of employee well-being.

Further, there are examples of organizations that have attained a high level of both performance and well-being. For example, the description of Southwest Airlines (SWA) in Milliman, Ferguson, Trickett, and Condemi (1999) indicates that SWA has attained both performance and well-being. Milliman et al. (1999) note the good performance record of SWA in terms of profitability and customer service. At SWA, one of the indicators of the high level of employee performance is that SWA has one of the lowest labor cost per mile flown among major airlines and that employees have been instrumental in SWA's receipt of quality awards (Milliman et al., 1999). Thus, high performance of individual employees seems to be a factor facilitating high profitability and customer service levels as organizational level performance indicators of the airline. The description of SWA in Milliman et al. (1999) also mentions low employee quitting rates and high employee satisfaction levels and SWA's consistent presence in the list of 100 best companies to work for in the USA. These can be regarded as indicators of employee well-being. Thus, SWA serves as an example of organizations that attain both employee performance and well-being.

The feasibility of attaining both employee performance and well-being is also reflected in organization-level data, which indicate that organizations in which employees have a high level of well-being tend to have a high level of organizational performance. An article titled "Happy Employees Mean Healthier Investor Returns" (*Economic Times*, July 20, 2016) provides the following information. *Economic Times* Great Places to Work study for 2016 ranked 100 organizations, of which 28 organizations were listed in stock markets. Stocks of 71% of these 28 companies have performed at a higher level than the indices of their respective sectors for the last one, three, and five years (*Economic Times*, July 20, 2016).

The feasibility of attaining both employee performance and well-being is noted in Harter et al. (2002). Gallup Workplace Audit (GWA) items, reported in Harter et al. (2002, p. 269), reflect positive perceptions of organizational conditions or positive experiences of employees in the workplace. Harter et al. (2002, p. 269) note that the GWA items are the antecedents of employees' positive affective reactions such as job satisfaction. Harter et al. (2002) view GWA items as measuring employee well-being. Harter et al. (2002) report that the data from thousands of business units from different organizations revealed an empirical relationship between employee well-being, measured in terms of GWA items, and business unit productivity. These empirical findings also indicate that it is feasible for work units to simultaneously attain employee performance and well-being.

Action areas covered in this book for enhancing employee performance and well-being

As employee performance and employee well-being are two significant outcomes for an organization, it becomes important for managers and organizations to consider the ways in which both these outcomes can be enhanced in an organization. While various action inputs are available to enhance employee performance and well-being, the following chapters focus on four inputs, namely transformational leadership, organizational justice, organizational support, and workplace spirituality. Out of several action inputs, only these four are covered in the subsequent chapters for four reasons outlined below.

First, all these four areas have emerged in the organizational behavior discipline only relatively recently. Transformational leadership came into organizational behavior in 1985 through the pioneering work of Bass (1985). Organizational justice in organizational behavior emerged around 1980 based on the following. The organizational justice label collectively refers to three forms of justice –distributive justice, procedural justice, and interactional justice. Further, procedural justice seems to have come into OB around 1983 (Pawar, 2009), and the interactional justice component of organizational justice came into OB even later, as Masterson, Lewis, Goldman, and Taylor (2000, p. 738) indicate that Bies and Moag (1986), as cited in Masterson et al. (2000), coined the term interactional justice. Organizational support came into organizational behavior through the pioneering work of Eisenberger, Huntington, Hutchison, and Sowa (1986). Workplace spirituality, as an area of systematic research, emerged around the 1990s (Pawar, 2009).

Second, these four areas have received considerable research attention over the period and have withstood the test of empirical examination. For example, there are meta-analysis studies integrating the empirical findings in the area of transformational leadership (Lowe, Kroeck, and Sivasubramaniam, 1996), organizational citizenship behavior (LePine, Erez, and Johnson, 2002), organizational support (Rhoades and Eisenberger, 2002), and organizational justice (Cohen-Charash and Spector, 2001). While workplace spirituality is the most recent of these four areas, the review of literature in this area by Karakas (2010, p. 89) indicates that "about 140 articles on workplace spirituality" and a review of empirical studies in workplace spirituality (Benefiel, Fry, and Geigle, 2014) is also available. This indicates that there is a considerable amount of literature, including empirical literature, even in the area of workplace spirituality.

Third, there is a common mechanism among them as each one of them seeks, in varying degrees and forms, to induce employees to transcend their self-interests in the process of forming positive orientations toward and making contributions to an organization (Pawar, 2009). In each of these areas, the specific mechanisms of their effects on employee performance and well-being are labeled differently. For example, procedural justice seeks to induce employees' positive concern for organizations through the mechanism often referred to as group value model, which suggests that the experience of procedural justice by employees symbolically conveys to them that they are valued by the group and then, in turn, they value the membership of the organization or the group (Lind and Tyler, 1988; Pawar, 2009). Transformational leadership is suggested to induce extra effort from subordinates through various mechanisms, including that of the subordinates' transcendence of their self-interests (e.g., Bass, 1985).

Fourth, each of these four areas can, as outlined in the subsequent chapters, enhance both employee performance and well-being. For example, the meta-analysis of organizational justice (Cohen-Charash and Spector, 2001) includes outcomes of justice that reflect both employee performance and employee well-being. This is an important positive feature of these four action areas because, as outlined earlier in this chapter, it is challenging to simultaneously enhance the twin outcomes of employee performance and well-being because there is a likelihood that improving one of these two outcomes may undermine the other. Similarly, while one of the challenges in enhancing employee well-being is that enhancing one form of employee well-being can lower another form of well-being (Grant et al., 2007), one of the action areas covered in the book – workplace spirituality – has been empirically found to have positive association with multiple forms of employee well-being. Specifically, there is evidence that employee experience of workplace spirituality has a positive association with employees' emotional well-being, psychological well-being, social well-being, and spiritual well-being (Pawar, 2016). Further, transformational leadership, which is one of the four action areas covered in the book, has been found to have a positive relationship with employees' mental well-being and spiritual well-being (McKee, Driscoll, Kelloway, and Kelly, 2011).

The above four reasons suggest that the application of inputs from these areas will help apply relatively recent empirically based knowledge for enhancing employee performance and well-being. The presence of the common mechanism of employees' self-interest transcendence in them also suggests that they can be implemented together to produce a complementary effect. The likely effect of their simultaneous application is outlined in Figure 3.1 from Pawar (2015, p. 331), reproduced as follows in a revised form.

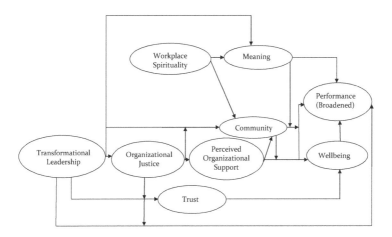

Figure 3.1 Interconnected effects of leadership, justice, support, and workplace spirituality on employee performance and well-being

Source: Reproduced and adapted with permission from Pawar (2015), p. 331

References

Bass, B. M. 1985. *Leadership and Performance Beyond Expectation.* Free Press: New York, NY.

Benefiel, M., Fry, L. W. and Geigle, D. 2014. Spirituality and religion in the workplace: History, theory, and research. *Psychology of Religion and Spirituality*, 6(3): 175–187.

Bies, R. J. and Moag, J. S. 1986. Interactional justice: Communication criteria of fairness. *Research on Negotiation in Organizations*, 1: 43–55.

Borman, W. C. and Motowidlo, S. J. 1997. Task performance and contextual performance: The meaning for personnel selection research. *Human Performance*, 10(2): 99–109.

Cohen-Charash, Y. and Spector, P. E. 2001. The role of justice in organizations: A meta-analysis. *Organizational Behavior and Human Decision Processes*, 86: 278–321.

Eisenberger, R., Huntington, R., Hutchison, S. and Sowa, D. 1986. Perceived organizational support. *Journal of Applied Psychology*, 71: 500–507.

Fry, L. W. and Slocum, J. W, Jr. 2008. Maximizing the triple bottom line through spiritual leadership. *Organizational Dynamics*, 37(1): 86–96.

Gavin, H. G. and Mason, R. O. 2004. The virtuous organization: The value of happiness in the workplace. *Organizational Dynamics*, 33(4): 379–392.

Grant, A. M., Christianson, M. K. and Price, R. H. 2007. Happiness, health, or relationships? Managerial practices and employee well-being tradeoffs. *Academy of Management Perspectives*, 21(3): 51–63.

Happy employees mean healthier investor returns. *Economic Times*, July 20, 2016.

Harter, J. K., Schmidt, F. L. and Hayes, T. L. 2002. Business-unit-level relationship between employee satisfaction, employee engagement, and business outcomes: A meta-analysis. *Journal of Applied Psychology*, 87(2): 268–279.

Harter, J. K., Schmidt, F. L. and Keyes, C. L. M. 2002. Well-being in the workplace and its relationship to business outcomes: A review of the Gallup studies. In C. L. M. Keyes and J. Haidt (Eds.), *Flourishing: The Positive Person and the Good Life* (pp. 205–224). American Psychological Association: Washington, DC.

Karakas, F. 2010. Spirituality and performance in organizations: A literature review. *Journal of Business Ethics*, 94(1): 89–106.

LePine, J. A., Erez, R. A. and Johnson, D. E. 2002. The nature and dimensionality of organizational citizenship behavior: A critical review and meta-analysis. *Journal of Applied Psychology*, 87: 52–65.

Lind, E. A. and Tyler, T. R. 1988. *The Social Psychology of Procedural Justice.* Plenum: New York, NY.

Lowe, K., Kroeck, K. G. and Sivasubramaniam, N. 1996. Effectiveness correlates of transformational and transactional leadership: A meta-analytic review. *Leadership Quarterly*, 7: 385–425.

Masterson, S. S., Lewis, K., Goldman, B. M. and Taylor, M. S. 2000. Integrating justice and social exchange: The differing effects of fair procedures and treatment on work relationships. *Academy of Management Journal*, 43(4): 738–748.

McKee, M. C., Driscoll, C., Kelloway, E. K. and Kelley, E. 2011. Exploring linkages among transformational leadership, workplace spirituality and well-being in health care workers. *Journal of Management, Spirituality and Religion*, 8(3): 233–255.

Milliman, J., Ferguson, J., Trickett, D. and Condemi, B. 1999. Spirit and community at Southwest Airlines. *Journal of Organizational Change Management*, 12(3): 221–233.

Narasimham, M. 1991. *Report of the Committee on the Financial System.* Reserve Bank of India. Bombay, India.

Pawar, B. S. 2009. Some of the recent organizational behavior concepts as precursors to workplace spirituality. *Journal of Business Ethics*, 88: 245–261.

Pawar, B. S. 2015. Enhancing research-teaching link in organizational behavior: Illustration through an actual example. *The International Journal of Management Education*, 13: 326–336.

Pawar, B. S. 2016. Workplace spirituality and employee well-being: An empirical examination. *Employee Relations: The International Journal*, 38(6): 975–994.

Rhoades, L. and Eisenberger, R. 2002. Perceived organizational support: A review of the literature. *Journal of Applied Psychology*, 87(4): 698–714.

Wilson, M. G., DeJoy, D. M., Vandenberg, R. J., Richardson, H. A. and McGrath, A. L. 2004. Work characteristics and employee health and well-being: Test of a model of healthy work organization. *Journal of Occupational and Organizational Psychology*, 77: 565–588.

Chapter 4

Traditional approaches to enhancing employee performance and well-being

Scientific management approach

The scientific management approach evolved around the end of the 19th century from the work of Frederick Winslow Taylor. This approach's philosophy had two elements – that the true interests of management and of labor were convergent and that all decisions concerning the work should be made based on science and not on rules of thumb (Taylor, 1911/2007, p. 7, 17). The second of these two elements – emphasis on scientific facts as the basis of decisions – seems to have given the label "scientific management" to this approach. This approach included the techniques of time and motion study, standardization, specialization, assignment of work to individuals, production quota specification for a day's work, piece-rate-based pay, scientific selection of employees, and training of employees (e.g., Locke, 1982; Taylor, 1911/2007). Collectively, these techniques form an approach in which time and motion study examines detailed movements in each job and, based on the optimal way of performing those movements, the overall time and an appropriate method for performing the job are identified. This method then is standardized and is to be followed by each employee. Each employee performs a limited range of operations or jobs, which constitutes his/her specialization. There is some evidence suggesting that the implementation of the scientific management approach resulted in considerable improvement in employee productivity in terms of the production output generated by employees (e.g., Taylor, 1911/2007, p. 42). Some of the features of the scientific management approach are depicted in Figure 4.1.

This approach focused on employees' task performance and did not consider the contextual performance contributions of employees.

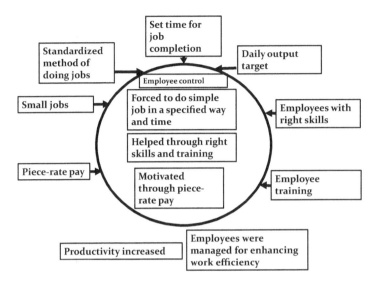

Figure 4.1 Some features of the scientific management approach

Source: Partly based on various works including Locke (1982) and Taylor (1911/2007)

This approach's techniques of short working hours and rest pauses along with piece-rate-based pay suggest that this approach can enhance employees' physical well-being, but it does not seem to have an explicit focus on other forms of well-being such as employees' emotional well-being, psychological well-being, social well-being, and spiritual well-being.

Human relations approach

While the scientific management approach of around the 1890s focused on individual assignment of work, the human relations approach focused on the benefits for employees of the social or informal groups at work and of the attention and consideration provided by the supervisors. In the human relations approach, it was recognized that employees are "social creatures" in addition to having economic needs and hence they want their opinions and feelings to be considered; like to have belongingness, participation, recognition, praise, positive relations with supervisors (Roethlisberger, 2004, p. 261–62). Thus, the human relations approach brought out the positive consequences of treating employees as human beings, requiring attention and consideration, and as social beings, requiring the membership and acceptance of their informal work groups. Thus, it may be said that while the scientific management approach focused on obtaining the maximum possible efforts from employees based on scientific decision-making about employee skills, methods, targets, and pay (e.g. Taylor, 1911/2007), the human relations approach focused on obtaining employees' cooperation with management and employees' participation and support at workplace (e.g., Gillespie, 2004, p. 392-393) using the "techniques of personnel counseling and supervisory training".

Thus, the scientific management approach focused on the technical, economic, and effort side of the work, and the human relations approach focused on the emotional and social side of the work. The actions adopted for this included using supervisors with human relations skills or the skills of being friendly and approachable with employees, and listening to and counseling employees (Wren, 1987). The supervisory approach of listening and being considerate to employees also provided employees some sense of participation. Such actions included in the human relations approach are likely to fulfill employees' social needs (Wren and Greenwood, 1998). Outcomes of this were expected to be enhanced employee cooperation with management, acceptance of organizational authority, morale or satisfaction, and productivity (Wren, 1987).

The human relations approach reflected that the view that a happy worker is a productive worker, and the term "happiness" could be interpreted as satisfaction (e.g., Organ, 1977). Satisfaction forms a positive form of emotion with a moderate level of arousal, and there are many other emotions varying in the direction of emotions – positive or negative – and level of arousal – high or low – in emotional well-being (e.g., Warr, 2005). The human relations approach, with its focus on happiness or satisfaction, can be said to have focused on a part of emotional well-being. Further, with its focus on providing employees a sense of belonging in the informal groups and the organization, it seems to have also focused on employees' social well-being. Thus, the human relations approach seems to have included in its focus a part of emotional well-being and social well-being but not the other forms of employee well-being, such as physical, psychological, and spiritual well-being. Further, while the descriptions of the human relations approach (e.g., Wren, 1987) indicate its likely contribution to enhanced employee productivity, these descriptions do not explicitly refer to non-task contributions of employees for the benefit of the organization. Thus, on the performance side, the human relations approach can be viewed as focusing mainly on employees' task performance and not on employees' contextual performance.

The employee happiness-productivity relationship was suggested in the human relations approach (e.g., Organ, 1977), where happiness was considered to be employee satisfaction. In a recent view (Gavin and Mason, 2004), employee happiness–productivity relationship is again suggested, but happiness is suggested to be coming from virtuous conduct and not from the pursuit of pleasure or material satisfaction. Employee freedom, knowledge, and virtue are suggested to be facilitating employee happiness and productivity (Gavin and Mason, 2004). Thus, while the utility of employee happiness in enhancing employee performance, as suggested in the human relations approaches, is noted (Organ, 1977), the need for focusing on a different form of happiness coming from employee knowledge/competence is also noted in the recent literature (e.g., Gavin and Mason, 2004).

The above brief description of the human relations approach indicates that it focused mainly on task performance and not on contextual performance of employees. The description also suggests that the human relations approach indirectly sought to address employees' emotional well-being and social well-being but not the other well-being forms of physical well-being, psychological well-being, and spiritual well-being. Thus, the human relations approach focused on a part of employee performance and employee well-being.

Employee participation

Hawthorne studies suggested that providing employees participation might be a way of enhancing employee performance and inducing acceptance of organizational policies (Wagner III, 2009, p. 446).

Employee participation provision can occur through several arrangements. Lawler and Mohrman (1987) note quality circles, task forces, work teams, and business teams as various arrangements for employee involvement. These employee involvement arrangements can provide various degrees of participation, ranging from joint involvement of employees with management to complete involvement of employees alone (Lawler and Mohrman, 1987). These could also vary in terms of the matters in which involvement is provided to employees; employees could be provided involvement in deciding work procedures, managing a performance unit, designing a performance unit and its context, or formulating organizational strategies (Lawler and Mohrman, 1987).

In principle, from providing employees participation, various positive outcomes are likely to come, such as improved employee satisfaction, enhanced acceptance of management decisions, and improved employee performance. However, empirical evidence, summarized through a meta-analysis of the findings of individual studies, suggests that the correlations of employee participation with employee performance and satisfaction, are around 0.11 (Wagner III, 2009, p. 447). This indicates that changing employee participation levels is likely to explain only about a 1% associated change in employee performance or satisfaction (Wagner III, 2009, p. 447). From this, employee participation comes out as an approach with very limited utility for enhancing employee performance and satisfaction or well-being.

Job enrichment

Job enrichment focused on enhancing employee motivation by providing employees positive experiences from the very act of performing a job. Herzberg (1968) suggested that providing employees feelings of challenge, growth, recognition, responsibility, etc. could motivate employees to put in more effort for doing the job. Herzberg (1968) proposed that job features, such as making an employee do a natural unit or whole piece of a job, removing the higher authority's or supervisor's controls over the employees, and providing employees an opportunity to do more difficult operations and use a broad range of skills, could provide to employees the feelings from the job which would enhance employees' motivation for doing the job. Building these and such features in a job is referred to as job enrichment (Herzberg, 1968). Herzberg (1968) reports a simple experiment in which he changed the jobs of a group of employees by removing some of the supervisory controls, making employees responsible for the job completion, providing employees a larger work unit to perform, etc. A few months after making these changes, the performance and attitudes toward the job of employees in this group showed considerable improvement.

This approach is in contrast with the scientific management approach (e.g., Taylor, 1911/2007), in which the jobs were made small to facilitate employee specialization and application of a limited range of employee skills and were designed to be performed in a standard way, and in which control in terms of designing the work methods and setting individual employees' production targets remained with the management. Thus, in some ways, this approach sought to reverse some of the features of the scientific management approach. It undermined the importance of pay as a motivator, whereas in the scientific management approach the piece-rate pay system was considered to be a source of employee motivation for putting in extra effort on the job.

Job characteristics model

An extension of the job enrichment approach is reflected in the job characteristics model. The job characteristics model (Hackman and Oldham, 1975, 1976) suggests that certain characteristics of a job result in positive psychological states in employees performing the job and then, as an outcome, give rise to employee satisfaction, enhanced intrinsic motivation, and performance. The job characteristics included in this model fall into three categories, in which each category is suggested to result in a specific psychological state, as described below.

The job characteristics model (Hackman and Oldham, 1975, 1976) suggests the following pattern of relationships. If an employee's job allows him/her to apply a variety of skills for completing it, forms a whole and identifiable unit, and has significance in terms of its important consequences for others, the employee is likely to experience the psychological state of meaningfulness. If an employee has autonomy in performing the job, then he/she experiences the psychological state of feeling responsible for the job. If an employee receives feedback about how well he/she is doing the job, then he/she experiences the psychological state of having the knowledge of results. These three psychological states of meaningfulness, felt responsibility, and the knowledge of results then give rise to employee satisfaction, intrinsic motivation, and performance. A very early test of this model (Hackman and Oldham, 1975) revealed that the job dimensions in the model relate to employee psychological states and to outcome variables of general satisfaction, growth satisfaction, internal work motivation, performance, and absenteeism in a manner consistent with the relationships between job dimensions and the variables specified in the model. Empirical evidence is generally supportive of this approach (Glick, Jenkins, and Gupta, 1986).

Job satisfaction, which is suggested to be an outcome in the model, reflects only one of the several emotions covered in emotional well-being. Job satisfaction covers the positive emotion of a moderate level of arousal and thus leaves out other positive emotions of low and high arousal levels. Thus, job satisfaction, which is a well-being-related outcome variable in the job characteristics model, covers only a part of emotional well-being. Further, one of the six components of psychological well-being is autonomy (e.g., Ryan and Deci, 2001) and thus the job characteristic of autonomy included in the model implies that the model also has the potential to partly enhance employees' psychological well-being. Thus, while a part of emotional and psychological well-being is indirectly covered in the model, social well-being and spiritual well-being forms are not explicitly covered in the model. Further, there is no explicit reference to employees' contextual performance as an outcome of the model. Thus, this approach's explicit focus is on only a limited form of employee performance and well-being.

Goal-setting approach

The goal-setting approach (e.g., Latham and Locke, 1979) involves setting difficult rather than easy and specific rather than vague task performance goals for employees. For example, asking employees to do as much as they can or do their best provides them vague and not difficult goals. The goal-setting approach is based on the assumption that conscious goals influence human behavior (Locke and Latham, 2002). It also is based on the premise that while needs and values can motivate human behavior, goals are the most immediate and alterable regulators of human behavior (Locke, 1978). Hence, the goal-setting approach seems to promote an employee's self-regulation through goals. Employees can regulate their functioning by tracking their progress toward goals when goals are specific. This self-regulation can be a source of employee motivation.

Specific and difficult goals for an employee's task influence an employee's task-directed behavior in several ways. Specific and difficult goals for an employee help the employee to focus attention, apply a higher level of effort, adjust his/her task behaviors based on the extent of goal attainment, and persist in putting in efforts until the goals are attained (Locke and Latham, 2002). These features of functioning coming from difficult and specific goals can induce a higher level of employee performance than when the goals are easy and vague.

Difficult and specific goals result in a higher performance level when certain other conditions are present. Such conditions include employees' commitment to the goal, the availability to employees of feedback on the extent of goal attainment, and a manageable level of task complexity (Locke and Latham, 2002). Further, commitment to goals can be enhanced by factors such as the provision of rewards, training, and support and the emergence of competition among employees (Latham and Locke, 1979; Locke and Latham, 2002).

The goal-setting approach described earlier seems simple. As a result, a question may be raised as to whether setting specific and difficult goals on a task for employees will result in a higher performance level for the employees. Latham and Locke (1979, p. 75) present a list of ten studies involving the use of the goal-setting approach. The tasks covered in these studies are varied, and study durations range from one to two days to two years. Latham and Locke (1979, p. 75) indicate that the median level of performance improvement in these ten studies was 17%. Thus, approximately an average performance improvement in these ten studies was 17%. An even stronger evidence base exists in that about 500 studies conducted on various types of jobs have shown that employee performance level under specific and difficult goals provision is higher than under vague and easy goals provision (e.g., Latham, 2003). This is an extensively researched area with over a thousand articles written on it (Latham and Pinder, 2005, p. 496). Thus, goal-setting seems to be an effective approach for enhancing employee performance. However, its focus seems to be mainly on task performance. Further, as goal-setting can facilitate the enhancement in employee self-efficacy (Locke and Latham, 2002), it is likely to enhance employees' psychological well-being. Thus, the goal-setting approach seems to have its main focus on task performance and not on contextual performance and on only some forms of employee well-being.

Work teams or self-managed work teams

A work group is set of individuals who are interdependent because of their tasks, regard themselves as a social unit, are a part of a context such as an organization, and generate outcome that affects others (Guzzo and Dickson, 1996, p. 307). Guzzo and Dickson (1996) note that in the present time, usually the term "teams" is used instead of the term "groups," and this description of a work group also adequately describes various teams carrying different labels and self-managed teams.

A self-managed team is a team in which employees take responsibility for their work, for monitoring their performance, and for adopting actions for solving performance problems (Wageman, 1997). Several features of work teams have been suggested to facilitate team effectiveness. These features include collective purpose; clear direction; specific goals; adequacy of skills, resources, and information; development of group roles; collective rewards; and a reasonable level of group cohesiveness (Guzzo and Dickson, 1996; Hackman and Wageman, 2009; Katzenbach and Smith, 1993; Wageman, 1997). Managing task conflict collaboratively and absence of relational or interpersonal conflict can also facilitate team performance (Weingart and Jehn, 2009).

While self-managed teams can potentially contribute to organizational performance and adaptability, many self-managed teams actually fail to do so, and hence evidence on their effectiveness is mixed (e.g., Wageman, 1997, p. 50). However, groups, teams, and self-managed work teams do not seem to have been linked to a broad range of outcomes such as multiple forms of employee well-being and employees' task performance and contextual performance. Thus, they can be viewed as an approach focused mainly on a limited form of employee performance and well-being.

Integrated view of some of the traditional approaches

Each approach described earlier seems to take specific types of actions in order to enhance employee performance and well-being, though it focuses, as outlined in the preceding part, on a limited part of employee performance and well-being. An integrated view of these approaches is depicted in Figure 4.2.

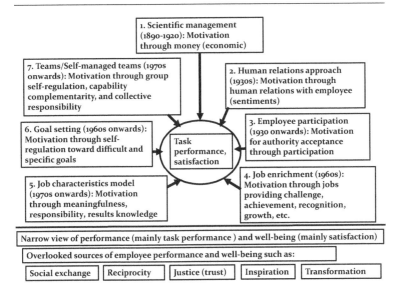

Figure 4.2 An integrated view of some of the traditional approaches

Source: The features of individual traditional approaches in the figure are partly based on descriptions in various works including Hackman and Oldham (1976), Herzberg (1968), Latham and Locke (1979), Latham (2003), Taylor (1911/2007), Wageman (1997), Wagner III (2009), and Wren (1987), and the contents in the preceding part of this chapter.

General remarks about the traditional approaches and the action inputs in the book

A few observations about the above outlined traditional approaches are as follows. First, these approaches focused mainly on employees' task performance and not on employees' contextual performance. Thus, the main performance-related outcome variable in these models or approaches has been employees' task performance. Second, the employee well-being-related outcome in these models has mostly been some form of employees' job satisfaction, which is only one part of the multiple forms of employee well-being. Thus, the traditional approaches seem to have focused on a narrow range of employee outcome variables. Third, the various work-related features covered in these models have not been systematically interlinked. Thus, an overall model for guiding multiple actions that collectively can enhance multiple forms of employee performance and well-being does not explicitly emerge from these individual approaches. In contrast, the proposed model used in this book to suggest the possible actions for enhancing employee performance and well-being overcomes all these three limitations associated with the traditional approaches. First, it focuses on both task performance and contextual performance of the employee as one of its outcome variables. Second, it focuses on multiple forms of employee well-being – physical, emotional, psychological, social, and spiritual – as another of its outcome variables. Employee job satisfaction forms only one part of one form – emotional well-being – of these multiple forms of well-being covered as one of the outcome variables in the model adopted in this book. Third, the various organizational features – transformational leadership, organizational justice, organizational support, and workplace spirituality – and associated actions for enhancing employee performance and well-being included in the model are interrelated in the model. These inputs and actions can collectively and in a mutually complementary way influence employee performance and well-being. Each of these features – transformational leadership, organizational justice, organizational support, and workplace spirituality – which can serve as the basis of possible actions for enhancing employee performance and well-being, is described in the subsequent sections of this book.

References

Gavin, H. G. and Mason, R. O. 2004. The virtuous organization: The value of happiness in the workplace. *Organizational Dynamics*, 33(4): 379–392.

Gillespie, R. 2004. Human Relations in Industry. In J. C. Wood and M. C. Wood (Eds.), George Elton Mayo: Critical Evaluation in Business and Management (Volume II, pp. 392–420). Routledge: New York, NY.

Glick, W. H., Jenkins, G. D. and Gupta, N. 1986. Method versus substance: How strong are underlying relationships between job characteristics and attitudinal outcomes. *Academy of Management Journal*, 29(3): 441–464.

Guzzo, R. A. and Dickson, M. W. 1996. Teams in organizations: Recent research on performance and effectiveness. *Annual Review of Psychology*, 47: 307–338.

Hackman, R. J. and Oldham, G. R. 1975. Development of the job diagnostic survey. *Journal of Applied Psychology*, 60(2): 159–170.

Hackman, R. J. and Oldham, G. R. 1976. Motivation through the design of work: Test of a theory. *Organizational Behavior and Human Performance*, 16: 250–279.

Hackman, R. J. and Wageman, R. 2009. Foster team effectiveness by fulfilling key leadership functions. In E. A. Locke (Ed.), *Handbook of Principles of Organizational Behavior* (pp. 275–293). John Wiley & Sons: West Sussex.

Herzberg, F. 1968. One more time: How do you motivate employees? *Harvard Business Review*, January–February: 53–62.

Katzenbach, J. R. and Smith, D. K. 1993. The discipline of teams. *Harvard Business Review*, 71: 111–120.

Latham, G. P. 2003. Goal-setting: A five step approach to behavior change. *Organizational Dynamics*, 32(3): 309–318.

Latham, G. P. 2009. Motivate employee performance through goal setting. In E. A. Locke (Ed.), *Handbook of Principles of Organizational Behavior* (pp. 171–178). John Wiley & Sons: West Sussex.

Latham, G. P. and Locke, E. A. 1979. Goal setting – A motivational technique that works. *Organizational Dynamics*, 68–80.

Latham, G. P. and Pinder, C. C. 2005. Work motivation theory and research at the dawn of the twenty-first century. *Annual Review of Psychology*, 56: 485–516.

Lawler, E. E. and Mohrman, S. A. 1987. Quality circles: After the honeymoon. *Organizational Dynamics*, 15(4): 42–54.

Locke, E. A. 1978. The ubiquity of the technique of goal-setting in theories of and approaches to employee motivation. *Academy of Management Review*, 3(3): 594–601.

Locke, E. A. 1982. The ideas of Frederick W. Taylor: An evaluation. *Academy of Management Review*, 7(1): 14–24.

Locke, E. A. and Latham, G. P. 2002. Building a practically useful theory of goal setting and task motivation: A 35-year odyssey. *American Psychologist*, 57(9): 705–717.

Organ, D. W. 1977. A reappraisal and reinterpretation of the satisfaction-causes-performance hypothesis. *Academy of Management Review*, 2: 46–53.

Roethlisberger, F. J. 2004. Human relations in industrial organizations. In J. C. Wood and M. C. Wood (Eds.), George Elton Mayo: Critical Evaluation in Business and Management (Volume I, pp. 261–267). Routledge: New York, NY.

Ryan, R. M. and Deci, E. L. 2001. On happiness and human potentials: A review of research on hedonic and eudaimonic well-being. *Annual Review of Psychology*, 52: 141–166.

Taylor, F. W. 1911/2007. *The principles of scientific management*. NuVision Publications: Sioux Falls, SD.

Wageman, R. 1997. Critical success factors for creating superb self-managing teams. *Academy of Management Executive*, 26(1): 49–61.

Wagner, J. A. III, 2009. Use participation to share information and distribute knowledge. In E. A. Locke (Ed.), *Handbook of Principles of Organizational Behavior* (pp. 445–459). John Wiley & Sons: West Sussex.

Warr, P. 2005. Work, well-being, and mental health. In J. Barling, E. K. Kelloway and M. R. Frone (Eds.), *Handbook of Work Stress* (pp. 547–573). Sage: Thousand Oaks, CA.

Weingart, L. R. and Jehn, K. A. 2009. Manage Intra-team conflict through collaboration. In *Handbook of Principles of Organizational Behavior* (pp. 327–346). John Wiley & Sons: West Sussex.

Wren, D. A. 1987. *The Evolution of Management Thought*. John Wiley & Sons: New York, NY.

Wren, D. A. and Greenwood, R. G. 1998. *Management innovators*. Oxford University Press: New York, NY.

Chapter 5

Transformational leadership for employee performance and well-being

Exercise 1

This exercise should be done before reading the chapter. You may have come across a leader for whom you worked or whom you have known (a manager, teacher, relative, friend) and whose: (a) subordinates/followers put in a lot of extra effort on the job, (b) subordinates/followers feel highly satisfied with the leader, and (c) work unit/group is highly effective. Recall any such specific leader and write down his/her name. Now, based on your recollection, comprehensively write down how the leader behaved toward his/her subordinates/followers and others in the organization. The work done on this exercise will be used at the end of the chapter to connect transformational leadership to the actual workplace.

What is leadership and why is it required in organizations?

Organizations can be viewed as systems that carry out coordinated implementation of activities required for organizational goal attainment (Selznick, 1948). An organization has its own goals to attain. A hospital may have treating a certain number of patients within a period as its goal. An educational institute may have the goal of annually passing a certain number of students with certain levels of education completed. While these examples of goals refer to the outcome produced by the organizations, ultimately, most organizations, and particularly commercial organizations, will have generating certain amounts of profits and sustaining oneself as its goals. Thus, at the ultimate level of organizational survival or at the operational level of producing a certain level of a particular kind of outcome, each organization has its own goals. If an organization does not satisfactorily attain its operational level goals, the possibility of its attaining the ultimate goal of self-sustenance may be adversely affected.

Organizations, in general, seek to attain their goals in a rational manner. This implies that organizations will comply with some norms of rationality in attaining their goals. Rationality may consist of two facets, namely instrumental rationality and economic rationality (Thompson, 1967). These two forms of rationality are, drawing partly on Thompson's (1967) view, briefly described below.

Instrumental rationality in an organization's actions would be present when the organization's actions are grounded in the correct belief that the action would produce the intended outcome. Specifically, an organization's goal-directed action would have instrumental rationality when the action is grounded in the correct belief that the action would facilitate the attainment of the goal. For example, if one is an a room that has only one door and if one's goal is to get out of the room, the action of walking in a direction away from the door does not have instrumental rationality, because it will not result in the attainment of the goal of getting out of the room.

Now let us consider the other form of rationality, namely economic rationality. An action has economic rationality if the action is the most economical means of attaining the goal for the attainment of which the action is used. For example, consider that a person is in an empty room that has only one door and his/her goal is to get out of the room. One possible action for the person is to take the position of facing the room's door and then walk toward the door along the shortest straight line between his/her position and the door. This action will have economic rationality, because it is the most economical action in terms of resources such as walking effort and time spent on attaining the goal of getting out of the room. However, consider a situation where the person turns his/her back to the door from the position where he/she is standing and then walks some distance away from the door and then, having gone farther from the door than where he/she initially was, he/she now turns around to face the door and walks toward the door. This action results in his/her taking more steps and spending more time for attaining the goal of getting out of the room than does the first action. Thus, this action does not have economic rationality, because the person performing it has not taken the shortest and the least time-consuming route to the door from his/her initial position.

If an organization considerably deviates from rationality in its actions toward the attainment of its goals, the organization is likely to carry out actions that are irrelevant to the attainment of its goals or actions that consume more than the minimally required resources. Such actions may affect the organization's survival because of its failure to attain its goals or its failure to maintain economic efficiency in attaining its goals.

An organization, in order to rationally carry out the actions required to attain its goals, requires several employees to carry out activities that fall in line with the organization's rational pursuit of its goals. However, just as an organization has its own goals and seeks to attain them through rationality, employees also have their own personal goals, needs, and preferences. Employees have their own self-interests and sentiments (e.g., Selznick, 1948) and may resist following the logic of rationality or logic of control imposed by an organization. As a result, when an employee joins an organization, his/her goals are likely to be focusing on fulfilling his/her needs by getting salary to support himself/herself and his/her family, to have some security and stability, to gain social recognition or respect by virtue of having a job, to have advancement in his/her career, etc. Thus, an organization's primary focus is likely to be on rationally attaining its goals, whereas the employees' primary focus is likely to be on fulfilling their own self-interest-based goals. In light of such divergence between the focus of an organization and its employees, employees of an organization may not naturally work toward the rational attainment of their organization's goals. Thus, it becomes necessary for the organization to deliberately influence employees to contribute to attaining organizational goals. An organization can exert such influence in a variety of ways.

One form of an organization's influence on employees could be in the form of the employment contract or terms of employment. Such a document may specify the main activities the employee is required to carry out and the likely deliverables expected from the employee, along with the monetary compensation and other benefits the employee will receive in return for fulfilling the activity requirements specified in the document. Performance monitoring, performance appraisal, performance appraisal-based pay raises, etc. can be viewed as some of the mechanisms used by an organization for influencing employees to contribute to the attainment of the organization's goals. This is one form of organizational influence.

Similarly, leadership in organizations is another form of an organization's influence over employees.

A leader in an organization "leads" employees toward the attainment of organizational goals. A leader identifies both employee needs as well as activities required from an employee for attaining the organizational goals. A leader also conveys to the employees, through his/her communication and behaviors, that he/she will fulfill certain employee needs to a certain extent when employees perform the activities required from them for the attainment of organizational goals. In this way, a leader influences employees to perform activities required for the attainment of organizational goals. Thus, a leader exercises influence over employees. However, this influence process used by a leader is not unilateral. It is a bilateral influence process, because a leader first understands the employee needs and conveys that certain employee needs will be fulfilled to a certain extent when employees carry out the activities required for the attainment of the organization's goals. Thus, a leader allows himself/herself to be influenced by the employees' needs in the process of influencing employees to work for organizational goals. Therefore, leadership can be viewed as a reciprocal influence process.

Different forms of leadership

Leadership, as an influence process, can take multiple forms. A manager can let the operations go on without any intervention as long as the required activities and results attainment are satisfactory. When the signals indicate that the required activities and result attainments are not satisfactory, the leader will intervene and take corrective actions. This is referred to as a management-by-exception form of leadership (Bass, 1990a; Bass, 1998; Den Hartog et al., 1997). While practicing this form of leadership, if a manager waits for signals of inappropriate functioning to come to him/her so that he/she could intervene with corrective actions, the form of leadership is referred to as management-by-exception in passive form (Bass, 1990a; Bass, 1998; Den Hartog et al., 1997). On the other hand, if a manager actively looks for signals of inappropriate functioning so that he/she could intervene with corrective actions, the form of leadership is referred to as management-by-exception in active form (Bass, 1990a; Bass, 1998; Den Hartog et al., 1997).

Another form of leadership is contingent reward leadership, in which a leader establishes a connection in the form of contingency between employee performance and employee rewards (Podsakoff, Todor, Grover, Huber, 1985, p. 26). This suggests a focus on rewarding subordinates based on their efforts or outcomes. The management-by-exception and contingent reward forms of leadership are both referred to as transactional leadership (e.g., Bass, 1990a). However, Wang, Oh, Courtright, and Colbert (2011, p. 234) note that contingent reward is the "most important indicator of transactional leadership.

Yet another form of leadership is transformational leadership. This leadership morally and motivationally elevates subordinates; it transforms the attitudes, beliefs, and values of subordinates (e.g., Bass, 1985; Burns, 1978). This form of leadership is described below by drawing upon various sources (e.g., Bass, 1985; Bass, 1990a; Burns, 1978; Carless, Wearning and Mann, 2000; Pearce and Sims, 2002; Podsakoff, McKenzie, Moorman, and Fetter, 1990; Rafferty and Griffin, 2004; Wang and Howell, 2010).

Transformational leadership: a brief description

A transformational leader engages followers in an interaction process in such a way that both the leader and his/her followers are raised to a higher level of morality (Burns, 1978, p. 20). This rise of the leader and the followers to a higher level of morality partly characterizes the transformation that is brought about by this leadership. A transformational leader embraces higher principles or moral values such as justice, peace, and freedom. A transformational leader's influence comes from the ideals, principles, and moral values which he/she adopts in his/her interactions with subordinates. This process of influence used by a transformational leader is in contrast with the transactional leader who exchanges rewards for the efforts of subordinates (e.g., Burns, 1978, p. 19). Burns (1978) included Mahatma Gandhi and Mao Tse-tung as examples of transformational leaders. The literature, some of which is cited below, suggests that transformational leadership can practiced through various behavior categories such as those outlined below.

The descriptions in the literature (e.g., Burns, 1978) suggest that one category of behavior includes influence through higher values. Add "Similarly, Pearce and Sim (2002, p. 192) included

focus on "higher purposes and ideals" as an aspect of transformational leadership. This category includes behaviors that
focus on ideals, moral values, and ethical aspects. A transformational leader can link ideals, moral values, and ethical aspects
with subordinates' jobs. He/she also can bring to the subordinates' attention the link between the subordinates' tasks and
the moral values, ideals, and ethical aspects. A transformational
leader could link higher or moral values such as diligence, honesty, truthfulness, service, and dedication with the subordinates'
task by pointing out to them that they can express such values
through their behaviors on the job.

Consider an example of a bank branch manager as a transformational leader. The branch manager could explain to a cashier that he/
she is not merely dispensing the cash but through cash dispensing, he/
she is rendering many forms of valuable help to the customers. He/she
could explain that a person withdrawing certain amount of cash may
go to the market to buy fruits, sell the fruits through the day for a little
higher price by going from one locality to another, and from the extra
amount earned through this selling activity, he/she would support his/
her family. Thus, cash dispensing by the cashier renders an important
service to the customer by helping him/her earn a livelihood for him/
her and his/her family. Thus, the values of serving others, altruism,
charity, etc. that can be furthered through the cashier's task of cash
dispensing are brought to the attention of the cashier. This enhances
the value of the cash-dispensing task in the mind of the cashier subordinate. Further, the branch manager could draw the subordinates'
attention to enhanced positive feelings such as satisfaction, joy, and
peace that he/she might experience because of doing the work of helping customers in various ways through his/her cash-dispensing task.
The cash-dispensing task becomes more meaningful and fulfilling
for the subordinate. This example illustrates how a transformational
leader, through his/her behaviors of linking higher values to subordinates' tasks, enhances the value of the task and task outcomes for his/
her subordinates.

The second category of behavior involves a leader's being becom-
ing an example for the subordinates (e.g., Carless et al., 2000; Podsakoff et al., 1990). Specific behaviors in this category could include
practicing in one's behavior the values (e.g., Carless et al., 2000)
or higher values which one seeks to link to subordinates' tasks.
Through such behaviors, a transformational leader is likely to be
trusted, respected, and admired. Further, as a transformational

leader links higher or moral values such as honesty, diligence, and dedication to the subordinates' tasks, he/she can serve as a role model for his/her subordinates by expressing such values through his/her own behavior. For example, a transformational leader can do his/her work honestly, diligently and with dedication and convey to the subordinates the joy he/she experiences by expressing such values through his/her work behaviors. This behavior category could reflect influence through value-based conduct.

The third category of behavior involves communicating to subordinates a vision of the future (e.g., Bass, 1985; Bass, 1990a; Carless et al., 2000; Pearce and Sims, 2002; Rafferty and Griffin (2004)). "A vision is a general transcendent ideal that represents shared values; it is often ideological in nature and has moral overtones (House, 1977)" (Kirkpatrick and Locke, 1996, p. 37). For example, a branch manager may tell his/her subordinates that if they all do their work by being aware of its larger significance of helping customers and while being honest, diligent, and dedicated in their work, their bank branch could become a service center or a charity center this behavior category is reflective of the "vision" and "inspirational communication" behaviors specified in Rafferty and Griffin (2004, p. 331–332). These behaviors are likely to make subordinates motivated and confident (e.g., Rafferty and Griffin, 2004). Thus, this category is likely to generate subordinates' energy toward vision accomplishment and reflects a leader's energizing behaviors.

The fourth category of transformational leadership behaviors involves intellectually enlivening subordinates (e.g., Bass, 1990a; Carless et al., 1990; Rafferty and Griffin (2004); Wang and Howell (2010)). A transformational leader encourages subordinates to think rationally, to question the old assumptions behind their work procedures, and to devise, solutions to the problems they may face (e.g., Bass, 1990a; Podsakoff et al., 1990; Rafferty and Griffin, 2004). In the traditional pattern of a manager-subordinate relationship, subordinates are used to receiving instructions from their manager and are likely to implement those with some degree of obedience and passivity. A transformational leader's above-described behaviors are likely to intellectually enliven their subordinates and hence generate the potential for a greater intellectual contribution from their subordinates. In this way, the traditional intellectual response pattern of subordinates is likely to be transformed, and the instruction-obedience form of a leader-subordinate relationship is likely to be transformed into one in which a subordinate become innovative and proactive in dealing with work-related problems.

The fifth category of transformational leadership behaviors involves a leader's respecting, recognizing, supporting, and developing each subordinate (e.g., Carless et al., 2000; Podsakoff et al., 1990; Rafferty and Griffin, 2004; Wang and Howell, 2010). Such personal attention and the associated behaviors that respect and develop subordinates of a leader towards his/her subordinates can help the subordinates to experience growth in their skills and potentials. Thus, subordinates can become capable of greater contribution to their work or work units.

The sixth category of transformational leader behaviors focuses on expressing that a high level of performance is expected from subordinates (e.g., Pearce and Sims, 2002; Podsakoff et al., 1990; Wang and Howell, 2010). Goal-setting theory (e.g., Locke and Latham, 2002) suggests that specific and difficult goals are more motivating than vague and easy goals. This suggestion emerging from goal-setting theory has been empirically examined and supported in several studies (e.g., Latham, 2003). Thus, a leader's high performance expectations from subordinates, when perceived as performance goals by subordinates, are likely to facilitate higher subordinate motivation. Similarly, the literature (e.g., Eden, 1984) on self-fulfilling prophecy suggests that a manager's holding high performance expectations from a subordinate is likely to result, through the effect of some intermediate steps, in high performance of subordinates. Consistent with these suggestions and findings in the literature, a transformational leader's expressing high performance expectations from subordinates is likely to enhance the performance motivation of subordinates.

There are multiple theoretical specifications of transformational leadership (e.g., Podsakoff et al., 1990). However, the above-described behaviors of transformational leaders seem to cover behaviors of transformational leaders specified in various theoretical specifications of transformational leadership as summarized in Podsakoff et al. (1990) and the perspectives described or reflected in other works (e.g., Burns, 1978; Carless et al, 2000; Pearce and Sims, 2002; Rafferty and Griffin, 2004; Wang and Howell, 2010). Based on the description of transformational leadership behaviors provided above by drawing on various works in the literature, a hypothetical example of a transformational leader is described below. Thereafter, the likely effects of the above-described transformational leader behaviors are described.

A hypothetical example of transformational leader behaviors

In light of the earlier provided descriptions, which are based on some of the relevant literature, of various forms of leadership, this section provides a hypothetical description of how these various forms of leadership, including transformational leadership, can be practiced. Consider a typical bank branch and the period of about the 1980s before the introduction of computerization in banks. Those days, manual entering of bank transactions in the ledger books was in use for recording customers' every transaction. Bank branches used to be open for customers to do their transactions between 10:30 a.m. and 2:00 p.m.; a 30-minute break was taken between 2:00 and 2:30 p.m., after which other work, such as posting transactions, was done. A bank branch was headed by a branch manager who was responsible for the branch's operations and performance. A bank branch's positions included substaff, cashier, clerk, and officer.

The cashier sat at the bank branch's cash withdrawal and deposit counter. Customers stood in a queue and carried with them the filled-in slips required for completing their transactions of cash withdrawal or cash deposit, as the case may be. When a customer's turn came at the front of the queue, he/she faced the cashier sitting at the cash counter and presented to the cashier his/her slip for cash withdrawal or deposit. The cashier checked the slip details for correctness, verified the appropriate records, counted cash, and provided cash to the customer as per the cash withdrawal amount mentioned in the slip. The cashier's job did not require a variety of skills, was monotonous, and did not provide much autonomy, because the activities needed to be performed in an established sequence. Thus, based on the job characteristics model (e.g., Hackman and Oldham, 1975), the intrinsic motivation coming from the job was likely to be low. Also, as pay level and benefits in the banks used to be moderate and not closely linked to the task performance level, the extrinsic motivation for the task itself was also likely to be low. Thus, the overall task motivation of the cashier was likely to be low. The branch manager could practice various forms of leadership. Each form of leadership might have different types of effects, as described below.

First, the branch manager could remain passive and manage only exceptions (problems or deviations) brought to his/her attention. He/she would sit in his/her office room, probably located at one end of the bank branch area, and keep doing his/her work at his/her desk. He/she might focus on responding to or making customer phone calls, read through and remark on various office reports, sign the papers that come from branch staff for his/her approval, deal with the customers who walk into his/her office for some queries, etc. While focusing on such work, he /she would not make any active effort to assess whether the operations in the branch and activities of the staff in the branch are being satisfactorily carried out. Thus, there is no possibility of proactively noticing and rectifying any inadequacy in staff activities. However, when someone or something brings to his/her attention that things have gone wrong, he/she would, upon being informed of such deviation, take a rectifying action. For example, if a customer were to come into his/her office room and complain that they had been is standing in the queue for a long time, but the queue was moving very slowly due to extremely slow work speed of the cashier, the manager might step out of the office and come to the branch operating area to see what the problem is and what can be done about it, so that the customers in the queue would receive service at a reasonable speed. In this approach, the manager exercises the act of influence only when things go wrong and the signals of the deviations or wrong occurrences are brought to his/her attention. This form of leadership is likely to induce only marginal extra effort from the branch employees and the cashier.

Second, the branch manager could actively detect and note exceptions (problems or deviations) and manage them by making a timely and corrective intervention. He/she would sit in his/her office room doing his/her work, such as receiving and making customer phone calls, studying bank operations reports, examining and signing the papers from the branch operations coming for his/her approval, dealing with queries of the customers who walk into his/her office, etc. While doing such routine works, he/she would periodically look through this office room glass at the cashier counter and branch operation area to assess whether the branch operations are happening satisfactorily. He/she might, for example, assess whether the queue at cashier counter is moving appropriately or see if there is any clamor in the operations area reflecting possibly some quarrel or severe expression of customer dissatisfaction or frustration. When such periodic assessments of his/her reveal to his/her signals of some inadequacies in the branch operations, he/she would intervene with actions to rectify the inadequacies. In this approach, the branch manager actively looks for signals of inadequacies or problems in the operations and, upon detecting such signals, he/she immediately intervenes with rectifying actions. The branch manager, in this approach, manages by dealing with the emergent exceptions or inadequacies and by promptly detecting and rectifying them, he/she actively monitors the work to look for and detect the signals of inadequacies or problems. Hence, this approach of the branch manager may be termed as "active management-by-exception." This approach might actively rectify the inadequacies and problems and hence might have greater efficacy than the "passive management-by-exception" approach in inducing extra effort from the branch employees and the cashier.

Third, the branch manager could lead employees by providing them rewards commensurate with and consequent to their work contributions or efforts. In this approach, the branch manager would identify what activities he/she wants the cashier to perform and clarify those activities to the cashier. The branch manager would also tell the cashier the kind of reward he/she would receive from the branch manager when those activities are satisfactorily performed by the cashier. The branch manager would then monitor the cashier's work and when that work is satisfactorily performed, the branch manager would provide the cashier the reward that was agreed upon for the performance of that work. This form of leadership promises and provides certain rewards to subordinates contingent upon their completing the work assigned to subordinates and hence is referred to as the contingent reward form of leadership. This leadership form's association with subordinates' perception of leader effectiveness is stronger than that of leadership which only focuses on correcting problems or deviations (e.g., Lowe, Kroeck, and Sivasubramaniam, 1996). In the present example of the bank branch, this suggests that this form of leadership of the branch manager is likely to be more effective than the leadership which only focuses on correcting problems or deviations.

Fourth, the branch manager could practice transformational leadership. In this approach, the branch manager would link moral values or higher values with the cashier's task. For example, the branch manager could link the moral or higher values of service, altruism, charity, honesty, and diligence to the cashier's task. He/she could explain to the cashier that a customer in the cashier's queue who withdraws a few hundred rupees might go to the wholesale fruit market to buy fruits and sell those fruits to households to earn a few hundred rupees more and use that additional earned amount to support his/her family. This would illustrate to the cashier that by performing his/her task, he/she is not only dispensing cash but is also helping customers earn their livelihood. Similarly, another customer in the cashier's queue might withdraw the cash to pay school fees of her son who might get access to the classroom contingent upon the school fees being paid on time. From these explanations provided by the branch manager, the cashier is likely to realize that he/she can render service, engage in altruism, and perform charity if he/she diligently does his/her cash-dispensing job. Thus, through the branch manager's communications with the cashier, the moral values or higher values of service, altruism, charity, and diligence are linked to the cashier's job. The branch manager, while practicing transformational leadership, could also explain to the cashier that working on the cash-dispensing task diligently and honestly helps him/her render more noble and valuable service to others. Through the realization of these aspects of his/her job, the cashier is likely to view his/her job as having high significance and thus is likely to put in extra effort and likely to experience a sense of meaning and high level of job satisfaction. These behaviors of the branch manager reflect his/her exercising influence through values in which he/she linked moral or higher values the cashier's (and other subordinates') tasks.

Further, the branch manager is likely to earn the cashier's (and other subordinates') trust, respect, and admiration by practicing the moral values or higher values such as service, altruism, charity, diligence, and honesty in his/her own functioning. As an illustration of the branch manager's practice of this transformational leadership behavior, consider the following example. Suppose a poor customer walks into the branch around the branch operations closing time and needs cash very quickly because he/she has to urgently reach his/her hometown within a few hours by catching the only bus for his/her hometown scheduled to leave in only a few minutes from the transport station. The customer tries to go to the cashier to speak to him/her, but the cashier, pointing to the long queue awaiting to be served in front of him/her, asks the customer to come as a part of the queue. This happens a couple of times and the branch manager, upon noticing this, could use multiple options, such as ignoring the occurrence, instructing the bank security guard to discipline the poor customer, or instructing the poor customer to follow the queue. However, rather than using such options, the branch manager goes to the operations area and politely asks the customer what the matter is. Based on the customer's narration, the branch manager learns that the customer's mother has suffered a major health problem in his/her hometown earlier that morning and the customer had received a message that a surgeon in the hospital in the hometown has asked for 20 thousand rupees to be deposited in the hospital before the end of the day so that he/she could arrange for and perform the required surgery on his/her mother the next morning. The surgeon also warned that her life would be at risk if the surgery is delayed beyond tomorrow morning. The only bus that goes to his/her hometown from this city will start in about 40 minutes, and it would take him/her about half an hour to reach the bus station. In these circumstances, it is necessary for him/her to get 20 thousand rupees cash from his/her account in less than ten minutes, but the queue in front of the only cashier is so long that if he/she becomes a part of the service queue then it will be impossible for him/her to be served by the cashier within ten minutes. Since the cashier has a long queue to serve and banking operations closing time is approaching, the cashier is not even listening to the circumstances of this customer. Upon coming to know these circumstances, the branch manager reflects for a few moments. He/she knows that he/she is working on preparing an important report required for the discussion in a meeting scheduled in about 40 minutes. It will take him/her about 20 minutes to complete the remaining work on the report, and he/she has planned to take his/her lunch in a shortened lunch break of only 20 minutes, which his/her will be able to get after completing the report and before the meeting commencement. He/she, however, decides to personally take it upon himself/herself to help this customer receive cash. Thus, as this example pertains to the period before bank computerization, he/she locates alternative documentation of customer balances and prepares the necessary slips in the process of working out an alternative procedure, which skips the cashier's involvement, to provide cash to the customer. While doing this, he/she realizes that the customer has only 18 thousand rupees to his/her credit. He/she then takes the personal risk to lend, as personal credit, the customer two thousand rupees out of his/her own pocket and thus gives him/her the entire required amount of 20 thousand rupees. As this work takes about 20 minutes, in order to avoid the customer's missing the bus, the branch manager provides him/her 50 rupees out of his/her own pocket and tells the customer to take a hired vehicle to reach the transport station in time to catch the only bus to his/her hometown. Now, as only about 20 minutes are left before the afternoon meeting, he/she has two choices – either to take his/her lunch quickly in 20 minutes and go for the meeting with an incomplete report or to skip his/her lunch to complete the report and then go to the meeting with the completed report – of which he/she chooses the option of skipping his/her lunch and completing the report for the meeting. He/she distributes his/her lunch box contents to the bank staff, skips his/her lunch, and still, after returning from the meeting, at the end of the day he/she is joyous. The bank branch staff's observation of this episode and his/her joy is likely to earn his/her the bank staff's trust, respect, and admiration because he/she has practiced moral or higher values of service, altruism, diligence, dedication, and commitment to one's duty in his/her own conduct and that also by his/her sacrifices of accepting additional hardship of personally rendering the cashier's service to the customer, giving money out of his/her own pocket, and skipping his/her lunch. Now, his/her appeals to the cashier (and other branch staff) to work for moral or higher values such as service, charity, altruism, honesty, and diligence would be received positively by them. It is likely that the cashier (and other bank staff) would feel proud to be associated with his/her, would want to emulate his/her and would feel an urge to please and obey his/her. These likely feelings of the subordinates are indicators of the branch manager's application of the influence of his/her value-based conduct on the cashier (and other branch staff) and of the successful operation of the branch manager's transformational leadership.

Continuing the same example, the branch manager could convey an attractive vision of what the bank branch would be if all of them work with the moral or higher values of service, charity, altruism, honesty, and diligence. For instance, the branch manager could communicate to the cashier (and other branch staff) that their bank branch would be a service center or a charity unit if all of them work with an attitude of service, charity, and altruism and work honestly and diligently in doing their bank branch tasks. He/she could also convey that then in the morning they would come to the bank branch eagerly looking forward to do meaningful work and in the evening leave the bank branch with a sense of joy and peace coming from doing meaningful work through the day. He/she could use various words and phrases to make this likely view of the branch as positive and attractive as possible to the cashier (and the other branch staff). Such enthusiasm and excitement experienced by the cashier (and the other branch staff) reflects the successful operation of the branch manager's transformational leadership behavior of vision provision and appealing communication which are likely to be instrumental in energizing subordinates.

The branch manager could also encourage the cashier to be intellectually active. For instance, he/she could tell the cashier that as there tends to be a heavy crowd and long cash counter queues during the days preceding festivals and the days following the first day of each month, the cashier could explore and devise new solutions in order to more effectively deal with customers during those days. The cashier, for example, might devise various ways of being more courteous or humorous or caring, depending on the customer profile, to make them feel more happy when they reach him/her at the front of the queue and thus neutralize the effect of the long queues and long waiting on those days. Such discovery and adoption of new and innovative solutions by the cashier (and other branch staff) reflect that they have been intellectually stimulated and more completely engaged at work through the branch manager's successful transformational leadership behavior of intellectual stimulation.

Further, the branch manager can also treat the cashier (and other branch staff) as an individual human being and respect and develop him/her. He/she could try to understand the distinct needs, values, capabilities, and potentials of the cashier and help the cashier to more adequately fulfill his/her needs and develop his/her capabilities and potentials. If, for example, the branch manager notices that the cashier has the capability to maintain good interpersonal relations with customers, the branch manager could tell this to the cashier and also tell him/her that if he/she does a part-time distance-learning mode diploma in customer relations or corporate relations, the cashier may be able to seek a transfer to those departments of the bank where he/she could have a better fit with those jobs and hence have greater fulfillment, job satisfaction, and career advancement in those departments. The branch manager could make further efforts to support the cashier's development by providing him/her information on such diplomas and encouragement to pursue them. The branch manager's development of the cashier would motivate the cashier to put in extra effort during the period when he/she is still in the branch and put in extra effort for the organization if and when he/she eventually completes the customer/corporate relations diploma and moves to the customer/corporate relations department of the bank. He/she is also likely to develop trust, respect, and admiration for the branch manager and likely to put in extra effort in his/her cashier's tasks in order to please and not to disappoint the branch manager. If all branch employees receive such support for their development from the branch manager, that would reflect the successful operation of the branch manager's respecting and developing subordinates form of transformational leadership.

The above hypothetical example of a branch manager's behaviors illustrates how some of the behaviors associated with transformational leadership can be practiced. It also illustrates the likely positive effects of transformational leadership on the subordinates. This example, focused on the branch work unit of banking industry, can serve as a guideline for managers in other departments, organizations, and industries to explore the possible actions through which they can practice transformational leadership in their own contexts.

The likely effects of transformational leader behaviors

Various transformational leadership behaviors were outlined earlier by drawing on the relevant literature. The likely outcomes of such behaviors are described below. When a transformational leader links moral values such as service, charity, altruism, honesty, and diligence to a subordinate's work, the work is likely to acquire moral significance. Subordinates performing such work are likely to receive the satisfaction coming from pursuing an activity which serves a moral purpose. The subordinates' work is likely to acquire some elements of nobility. This can enhance the subordinates' intrinsic satisfaction or joy coming from expending efforts on the work.

When a transformational leader performs behaviors which reflect the moral values that he/she seeks to link to subordinates' work, the subordinates are likely to develop positive regard for the leader. Such transformational leader behaviors include expressing moral values in one's conduct. Thus, when a transformational leader engages in behaviors that express moral values, at least three effects are likely to occur. First, a leader is likely to be respected, trusted, and admired. Second, the attempts of a transformational leader to link moral values and ideals to the subordinates' jobs are likely to make jobs appealing to the subordinates.

Third, subordinates are likely to feel proud to be associated with the leader and hence likely to be inclined to comply with the leader's appeals in order to receive the leader's approval or to not disappoint the leader.

When a transformational leader conveys an attractive vision (e.g., Rafferty and Griffin, 2004) of the future, which is directly or indirectly linked to the subordinates' tasks, the significance of the task for the subordinate is likely to be enhanced (e.g., Bass, 1985). This is because the task is likely to be seen as instrumental in attaining an attractive vision and hence expending efforts on the task is likely to provide a positive emotional experience to the subordinate. The symbolic and evocative communication used by a transformational leader in conveying a vision is likely to create enthusiasm and optimism for the subordinates. The enhancement of the subordinate's motivation through a leader's vision is also likely to occur for some other reasons. First, the vision of a transformational leader reflects shared aspirations of the subordinates (e.g., Avolio and Howell, 1992). Therefore, subordinates are likely to have high motivation to put in effort in the pursuit of vision because such efforts are also likely to facilitate the realization of their own aspirations. Second, the vision of a transformational leader tends to be idealized (Kirkpatrick and Locke, 1996), and a transformational leader raises the subordinates to a higher level of motives and values (Burns, 1978). Hence, the subordinates are likely to find the pursuit of ideals through vision or pursuit of idealized vision as motivating. The empirical evidence (e.g., Kirkpatrick and Locke, 1996) also supports the motivating effects on the subordinates of a leader's vision.

When a transformational leader serves as a role model (e.g., Podsakoff et al., 1990) of working toward the idealized vision and of following ethics and higher values in one's conduct, the subordinates' motivation for similar behaviors is also likely to be increased. Seeing others perform a task well enhances, under certain conditions, an observer's self-efficacy or belief that he/she can perform that task well (e.g., Bandura, 1977, cited in Stajkovic and Luthans, 1998). Subordinates of a transformational leader identify with a leader (e.g., Bass, 1990a, p. 21) and hence a transformational leader's behavior of working toward an idealized vision and of following ethics is likely to have an enhanced vicarious (observation-based) learning effect on the subordinates. Thus, subordinates are also likely to develop a belief that they can perform the behaviors expressing ethics and higher values.

When a transformational leader conveys high performance expectations Podsakoff et al. (1990) from his/her subordinates, their motivation is likely to increase for a variety of reasons. First, conveying high performance expectations may take the form of persuasion. Persuasion can enhance self-efficacy of the target of persuasion (Bandura, 1977, cited in Stajkovic and Luthans, 1998) and an individual's self-efficacy has a positive association with his/her performance (Stajkovic and Luthans, 1998). Thus, a transformational leader's conveying high performance expectations is likely to enhance, through the persuasion-self-efficacy link, the subordinates' performance on the vision-facilitating tasks. Second, a leader's high performance expectations are likely to provide challenging performance standards to the subordinates. Difficult and specific goals result in higher performance than easy and vague goals (e.g., Latham and Locke, 1979). Hence, a transformational leader's high performance expectations are likely to serve as difficult goals for the subordinates and thereby increase their performance.

When a transformational leader performs the behaviors which intellectually enliven his/her subordinates (e.g., Bass, 1990a, Rafferty and Griffin, 2004) they are likely to explore new and possibly improved ways of performing their tasks. This is likely to yield higher effort and also a new kind of intellectual effort from subordinates. The intellectual stimulation behavior of a transformational leader is also likely to promote greater problem-solving activity. Such effects of the intellectual stimulation behaviors of a transformational leader are thus likely to generate from the subordinates enhanced intellectual effort and new and improved ways of performing their tasks.

When a transformational leader performs behaviors which pay attention to each subordinate as a human being and which respect and develop each subordinate (e.g., Podsakoff et al., 1990), the subordinates' capabilities are likely to be developed and hence they are likely to have an enhanced performance potential. Further, this behavior is also likely to help the subordinates to realize their potential (e.g., Bass, 1995, p. 473) and to provide a growth experience to subordinates. Growth experience enhances intrinsic motivation. Hence, this behavior of a transformational leader is likely to enhance the subordinates' intrinsic motivation. Further, growth experience is also a part of psychological well-being (e.g., Ryan and Deci, 2001) and hence the individual consideration behavior of transformational leadership is likely to enhance subordinates' psychological well-being.

Collectively, these behaviors of a transformational leader are likely to have several effects. First, they are likely to broaden the range of motives or needs the subordinates seek to fulfill from work (e.g., Bass, 1990a, p. 21). Thus, the subordinates of a transformational leader are likely to pursue the fulfillment of higher needs and motives such as altruism and service. Thus, the subordinates are likely to follow a broader range of needs, including a higher level of needs, rather than just the lower level of needs such as the need for security. This is consistent with a transformational leader's intermediate effect on the subordinates' needs (e.g., Bass, 1985; Sparks and Schenk, 2001, p. 853). Second, because of the transformational leadership behaviors, the subordinates are likely to also see greater significance of their tasks because of the link of the tasks to ideals and to an attractive vision. This is consistent with a transformational leader's intermediate effect on the subordinates' experience of higher purpose in work (e.g., Sparks and Schenk, 2001). Third, transformational leader behaviors that induce subordinates to focus on group goals, pursue a higher level of needs and motives, and work toward a vision that reflects collective aspirations are likely to facilitate the subordinates' going beyond self-centered focus. This is consistent with one of the intermediate effects of transformational leadership described in the literature (e.g., Bass, 1990b, p. 853). Fourth, the subordinates are likely to put in a high level of intellectual effort and to have a high level of development in their capabilities. Fifth, the subordinates are likely to have a high level of self-confidence, commitment to a challenging and attractive vision, and the resulting high level of motivation on vision-directed tasks. The above literature-based description suggests several potential intermediate effects or mechanisms through which transformational leadership is likely to affect subordinates' outcomes such as performance and well-being. A considerable further illumination of such mechanisms comes from a very recent review by Ng (2017, p. 385, 386, 400), covering a large volume of research on transformational leadership performance outcomes, which found that transformational leadership influences employee performance outcomes through various mechanisms such as enhancing subordinates' job satisfaction and commitment to the organization, engagement and self-efficacy on the job, justice perceptions, identification with organization and leader, and social exchange with the organization and leader.

The above-described multiple likely effects may result in a higher level of employee effort, satisfaction, and well-being. These suggestions are consistent with empirical evidence which indicates that transformational leadership behaviors impact employee effort and in-role (task performance) as well as attitudes (Bass, 1995; Podsakoff et al., 1990). Transformational leadership behaviors also enhance employees' organizational citizenship behavior, job satisfaction, and trust in the leader (Podsakoff et al., 1990). Reviews of a large volume of empirical research by Judge and Piccolo (2004) and Ng (2017) have reported a positive relationship between transformational leadership and subordinates' job satisfaction. Transformational leadership also has a positive association with subordinates' perception of leadership effectiveness (Lowe et al., 1996). A recent review of a considerable amount of transformational leadership research over 25 years concluded that transformational leadership has a positive relationship with subordinates' task performance as well as contextual performance (Wang et al., 2011). A more recent assessment of Ng (2017, p. 385) is that there is solid evidence showing that the subordinates of transformational leaders are "more productive" when performance is assessed in terms of "in-role tasks, extra-role activities, or innovations". Further, the results of the meta-analytic review of Ng (2017, p. 394) also found that transformational leadership is positively associated with subordinates' task performance, organizational citizenship behaviors, and innovative behaviors. This supports that transformational leadership influences employees' task performance and contextual performance, and job satisfaction.

Based on the above discussion, literature, and empirical evidence, a few of the transformational leadership behaviors and some of the intermediate processes leading to various employee outcomes are outlined in Figure 5.1.

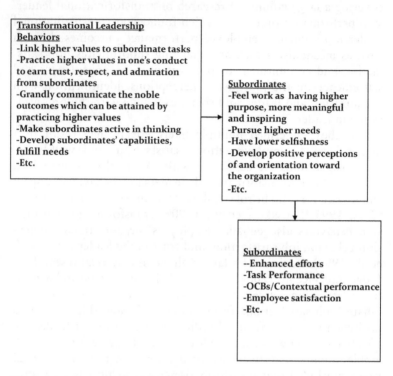

Figure 5.1 Some details of transformational leadership behaviors and outcomes

Source: Based on various sources including Bass (1985, 1995), Judge and Piccolo (2004), Lowe et al. (1996), Ng (2017), Podsakoff et al. (1990), Sparks and Schenk (2001), Wang et al. (2011)

Simultaneously performing transformational leadership behaviors with transactional leadership behaviors

Judge and Piccolo (2004, p. 757) note that among the various components of transactional leadership, the contingent reward component is the most effective one. The research findings indicate a high correlation between the contingent reward component of transactional leadership and transformational leadership (e.g., Goodwin, Wofford, and Whittington, 2001; Judge and Piccolo, 2004). These findings suggest that, in general, a manager who performs transformational leadership behaviors at a high level is also likely to perform transactional leadership behaviors at a high level. Thus, Bass (1995, p. 474) suggests that both transformational and transactional components are likely to be present in the best leaders.

However, transformational leadership is more effective than transactional leadership. For example, a greater percentage of transformational leaders than transactional leaders have subordinates who say they put in extra effort (Bass, 1990a). Similarly, transformational leadership has a stronger positive relationship than has transactional leadership with subordinates' extra effort, satisfaction with the leader, and perceptions of leader effectiveness (Yammarino and Bass, 1990). Further, transformational leadership adds to the contribution of transactional leadership to leadership effectiveness outcomes (Bass, 1995). For example, research findings indicate that transformational leadership adds to the effect of transactional leadership on the subordinates' evaluation of leadership effectiveness in terms of the extent to which a leader's unit fulfills its responsibilities and benefits the organization (e.g., Waldman, Bass, and Yammarino, 1990). However, recent findings from a large scale review of empirical research by Wang et al. (2011, p. 248) indicates that transformational leadership's such augmentation or additional or incremental effect beyond transactional leadership (measured using the contingent reward dimension) occurs only for employees' contextual performance and team-level performance. Recent research synthesis indicates that transformational leadership relates more strongly than does the contingent reward component of transactional leadership with some of the leadership effectiveness criteria, while the contingent reward component of transactional leadership relates more strongly than transformational leadership with some other leadership effectiveness criteria (Judge and Piccolo, 2004). However, aggregating across six leadership effectiveness criteria, transformational leadership relates slightly more strongly than does the contingent reward component of transactional leadership and considerably more strongly than do the other components of transactional leadership with the overall leadership effectiveness criteria (Judge and Piccolo, 2004). These findings, in general, suggest that a manager's transactional leadership behaviors induce a certain amount of leadership effectiveness and that the manager's transformational leadership can add to that base level for some aspects of some aspects of leadership effectiveness.

Thus, for a manager to induce extra effort from subordinates, it will be beneficial to practice both transactional leadership behaviors as well as transformational leadership behaviors. However, the distinct contribution of transformational leadership is that it can induce the moral and motivational elevation of subordinates (e.g., Burns, 1978) and induce subordinates to transcend self-interests (Bass, 1990a, p. 21). Moral and motivational elevation of subordinates and their transcendence of self-interests can bring various positive contributions to the organization. For example, when subordinates transcend their self-interests, they can perform organizationally beneficial extra-role behaviors, which are termed as organizational citizenship behaviors. Consistent with this, a positive relationship has been found between transformational leadership and subordinate organizational citizenship behavior (OCB) or contextual performance (e.g., Podsakoff et al., 1990; Ng, 2017; Wang et al., 2011). Transformational leadership's such likely outcomes for subordinates are reflected in Figure 5.1.

Exercises

Revisit and reflect on Exercise 1

At the beginning of the chapter, you were asked to describe the behaviors of a leader who induced considerable effort from his/her subordinates/followers and with whom his/her subordinates/followers were highly satisfied. Now, read through the description you wrote down. Assess how many of the behaviors you included in your description reflect endorsement, encouragement, or expression of moral values or higher values such as service, charity, altruism, honesty, diligence, punctuality, responsibility, fairness, and support. It is likely that such values are extensively reflected in the behaviors included in your description of the leader. On the other hand, aspects such promising financial rewards, comforts, etc. are not likely to be reflected much in the behaviors included in your description of the leader.

This pattern of the presence of aspects pertaining to the moral values or higher values and the absence of aspects pertaining to financial rewards and financial give-and-take indicates that the effective leader you have observed in the past had many features of a transformational leader and only a few features of a transactional leader. This pattern is similar to what the author has found in the exercise he/she does in his/her training sessions on transformational leadership. When the author asks managers to describe behaviors of a leader they had observed and who induced extra effort from subordinates and with whom the subordinates were satisfied, in general, managers provide behaviors that are somewhat similar to transformational leadership behaviors.

This pattern emerging from your work on Exercise 1 will reveal that an effective leader that you have seen in the past had many behaviors similar to the transformational leadership behaviors. From this, you will be able to see that transformation leadership behaviors can be practiced in workplaces similar to your own and by individuals like you. Further, you will realize that practicing transformational leadership behaviors can enhance one's leadership effectiveness.

Exercise 2

Consider the features such as the region of the country, industry, organization, and functional area in which you perform your role as a manager and also the kind of subordinates you have in terms of their culture, education levels, socio-economic backgrounds, etc. Also consider your own circumstances such as your personal background, life style, values, personal strengths, experience level, and tenure in the organization.

In light of these features, describe what specific behaviors you will perform to enhance your transformational leadership in your work unit. Be specific in describing: (a) the particular moral values or higher values (e.g., honesty, service, dedication) which you will link to your subordinates' tasks, (b) how you will communicate the link of these values to the subordinates' tasks, (c) what behaviors you will perform to express these values in your own work behaviors, (d) what behaviors you will perform to earn your subordinates' trust, respect, and admiration, (e) what vision you will have for your own work unit, (f) how you will communicate your vision for your work unit to your subordinates so that they see it as noble, attractive, and enthusiasm-enhancing, (g) what behaviors you will perform to intellectually activate your subordinates so that they can be innovative in thinking about and solving work-related problems, (h) how you will understand each of your subordinates as a human being, (i) how you will understand the needs, values, and potentials of each of your subordinates, (j) how you will help each of your subordinates to develop his/her capabilities and realize his/her potentials, (k) what behaviors you will perform to focus your subordinates' attention on your work unit's goals, (l) what behaviors you will perform in order to convey that you hold high performance expectations from your subordinates, and (m) what you will do to provide yourself as a role model for your subordinates.

References

Avolio, B. and Howell, J. 1992. The ethics of charismatic leadership: Submission or liberation? *Academy of Management Executive*, 43–54.

Bass, B. M. 1985. *Leadership and Performance Beyond Expectations*. Free Press: New York, NY.

Bass, B. M. 1990a. From transactional to transformational leadership: Learning to share the vision. *Organizational Dynamics*, 18(3): 19–31.

Bass, B. M. 1990b. *Bass & Stogdill's Handbook of Leadership*. Free Press: New York, NY.

Bass, B. M. 1995. Theory of transformational leadership redux. *Leadership Quarterly*, 6(4): 463–478.

Bass, B. M. 1998. *Transformational Leadership: Industry, Military, and Educational Impact*. Lawrence Erlbaum Associates: Mahwah, NJ.

Burns, J. M. 1978. *Leadership*. Harper & Row: New York, NY.

Carless, S. A., Wearing, A. J. and Mann, L. 2000. A short measure of transformational leadership. *Journal of Business Psychology*, 14: 389–405.

Den Hartog, D. N., Van Muijen, J. J. and Koopman, P. L. 1997. Transactional versus transformational leadership: An analysis of the MLQ. *Journal of Occupational and Organizational Psychology*, 70: 19–34.

Eden, D. 1984. Self-fulfilling prophecy as a management tool: Harnessing Pygmalion. *Academy of Management Review*, 9: 67–73.

Goodwin, V. L., Wofford, J. C. and Whittington, J. E. 2001. A theoretical and empirical extension to transformational leadership construct. *Journal of Organizational Behavior*, 22: 759–774.

Hackman, R. J. and Oldham G. R. 1975. Development of the job diagnostic survey. *Journal of Applied Psychology*, 60(2): 159–170.

Judge, T. A. and Piccolo, R. F. 2004. Transformational and transactional leadership: A meta-analytic test of their relative validity. *Journal of Applied Psychology*, 89(5): 755–768.

Kirkpatrick, S. A. and Locke, E. A. 1996. Direct and indirect effects of three core charismatic leadership components on performance and attitudes. *Journal of Applied Psychology*, 81: 36–51.

Latham, G. P. 2003. Goal-setting: A five step approach to behavior change. *Organizational Dynamics*, 32(3): 309–318.

Latham, G. P. and Locke, E. A. 1979. Goal setting – A motivational technique that works. *Organizational Dynamics*, (Autumn): 68–80.

Locke, E. A. and Latham, G. P. 2002. Building a practically useful theory of goal setting and task motivation: A 35-year odyssey. *American Psychologist*, 57(9): 705–717.

Lowe, K., Kroeck, K. G. and Sivasubramaniam, N. 1996. Effectiveness correlates of transformational and transactional leadership: A meta-analytic review. *Leadership Quarterly*, 7: 385–425.

Ng, T. W. H. 2017. Transformational leadership and performance outcomes: Analyses of multiple mediation pathways. *The Leadership Quarterly*, 28: 385–517.

Pearce, C. L. and Sims H. P., Jr. 2001. Vertical versus shared leadership as predictor of the effectiveness of change management teams: An examination of aversive, directive, transactional, transformational, and empowering leader behaviors. *Group Dynamics: Theory, Research, and Practice*, 6: 172–197.

Podsakoff, P. M., Todor, W. D., Grover, R. A. and Huber, V. L. 1985. Situational moderators of leader reward and punishment behaviors: Fact or fiction? *Organizational Behavior and Human Performance*, 34: 21–63.

Podsakoff, P. M., MacKenzie, S. B., Moorman, R. H. and Fetter, R. 1990. Transformational leader behaviors and their effects on followers' trust in leader, satisfaction, and organizational citizenship behaviors. *Leadership Quarterly*, 1(2): 107–142.

Rafferty, A. E. and Griffin, M. A. 2004. Dimensions of transformational leadership: Conceptual and empirical extensions. *The Leadership Quarterly*, 15: 329–354.

Ryan, R. M. and Deci, E. L. 2001. On happiness and human potentials: A review of research on hedonic and eudaimonic well-being. *Annual Review of Psychology*, 52: 141–166.

Selznick, P. 1948. Foundations of a theory of organizations. *American Sociological Review*, 13: 25–35.

Sparks, J. R. and Schenk, J. A. 2001. Explaining the effects of transformational leadership: An investigation of the effects of higher-order motives in multilevel marketing organizations. *Journal of Organizational Behavior*, 22: 849–869.

Stajkovic, A. J. and Luthans, F. 1998. Social cognitive theory and self-efficacy. *Organizational Dynamics*, 62–74.

Thompson, J. D. 1967. *Organizations in Action*. McGraw-Hill: New York, NY.

Waldman, D. A., Bass, B. M. and Yammarino, F. J. 1990. Adding to contingent-reward behavior: The augmenting effect of charismatic leadership. *Group & Organization Management*, 15(4): 381–394.

Wang, X. U. and Howell, J. M. 2010. Exploring the dual level effects of transformational leadership on followers. *Journal of Applied Psychology*, 95: 1134–1144.

Wang, G., Oh, I., Courtright, S. H. and Colbert, A. E. 2011. Transformational leadership and performance across criteria and levels: A meta-analytic review of 25 years of research. *Group & Organization Management*, 36(2): 223–270.

Yammarino, F. J. and Bass, B. M. 1990. Transformational leadership and multiple levels of analysis. *Human Relations*, 43(10): 975–995.

Chapter 6

Organizational justice for employee performance and well-being

Exercise 1

Kindly respond to the following statements to facilitate your reflection based on self-assessment.

1. Briefly write down in everyday common words what you understand by the term "justice."
2. One of your colleagues oversleeps and gets up very late in the morning at his/her home. What judgments will you form about this over-sleeping behavior and about him/her?
3. One of your colleagues deliberately works slow at work and hence some of the work that he/she should be doing gets passed on to you and your other colleagues. The subordinate, however, receives as much pay as you and your other colleagues do. What judgments will you form about this slow work and about him/her?
4. Vinod and Rajiv are two of your subordinates who work in the same unit and do similar jobs. The level of effort for both of them on the work tasks is mostly similar throughout the year. At the year's end, Vinod received a greater pay increase than did Rajiv. After knowing this pay increase difference, what would be Rajiv's (a) judgments about how he was treated, (b) feelings, and (c) reactions in terms of behaviors and effort levels at work?
5. Suppose Vinod has made many more positive extra work contributions than did Rajiv, such as making work improvement suggestions and training new workers. The pay increase was based on the effort on the work tasks and also such positive extra work contributions. This method is designed and used by the Human Resource Department and was applied to determining

the pay increase for all employees in the work unit. Now this is informed by the Human Resource Department to Rajiv. After knowing this information, what would be Rajiv's (a) judgments about how he/she was treated, (b) feelings, and (c) reactions in terms of behaviors and effort levels at work?

6. Suppose you, as the manager of Vinod and Rajiv, now spoke to Rajiv to provide an explanation to him/her for the reasons for his receiving a smaller amount of pay increase than Vinod. You told him/her that (a) you understand his hurt feelings, (b) the method of annual pay increase determination is designed and applied by the Human Resource Department and you have no control over it, (c) the method of pay increase determination is appropriate because it recognizes and encourages employees' positive contributions to the organization, and (d) you apologize to him/her that you have no authority to control this occurrence of lower pay increase for him/her. You explained this to Rajiv in a comprehensive manner and you were courteous, polite, respectful, and truthful with him/her while speaking to him/her on this aspect. Now, after this explanation incident, what would be Rajiv's (a) judgments about how he was treated, (b) feelings, and (c) reactions in terms of behaviors and effort levels at work?

Reflection on Exercise I

1. From your response to question 1, you would realize that by justice, we usually mean fairness, objectivity, impartiality, equality, evenhandedness, etc. These are common interpretations of the term justice. This will be discussed in the early part of the chapter.

2. Your response to question 2 is likely to suggest that you view the colleague's behavior as laziness and the colleague as lazy and lacking the virtue of self-restraint or self-discipline. However, you are not likely to view your colleague as doing injustice to anyone.

3. Your response to question 3 is likely to suggest that you view the colleague's behavior as unfair and the colleague as doing injustice or unfairness because he/she gets the same pay as other coworkers but he/she puts in less effort than other coworkers. From your responses to questions 2 and 3, you will realize that the presence of personal virtue and justice are two different aspects. A person may lack personal virtue (e.g., a lack

of self-discipline or self-restraint reflected in laziness), but this may not cause injustice to others. Thus, justice comes into play when one person's behavior is likely to adversely affect another person's interests or well-being in a manner that is not deserved by the circumstances about another person.

4. Your response to question 4 is likely to suggest that Rajiv feels that he did not receive the outcome (in this case the specific outcome of pay increase amount) which was deserved by his efforts on work tasks. His expectation of the outcome deserved by him/her is likely to be based on his knowledge of the outcome received by his coworker, Vinod. Thus, Rajiv's sense of having received less than the deserved outcome is based on his comparison of the outcome-efforts ratio of his own with that of his coworker. This comparison of outcome-efforts ratios that employees use to determine the fairness of their outcome is referred to as distributive justice, which is justice or justness in the distribution of outcomes. Your response is likely to suggest that Rajiv is likely to have various negative judgments, feelings, and reactions.

5. Your response to question 5 is likely to suggest that Rajiv's negative feelings and reactions are likely to become less negative after receiving the information that the method of pay raise determination was consistently applied to all employees. He is also likely to feel that there is some sort of fairness in the method or procedure of pay raise determination. The presence of features such as consistency in the application of decision-making procedures enhances employees' perception of procedural justice. This aspect of consistency of methods or procedures is used by employees as one of the indicators of procedural justice.

6. Your response to question 6 is likely to suggest that your providing comprehensive information and respectful interpersonal treatment to Rajiv is likely to make Rajiv feel that he has received some amount for fairness from you as a person (as distinct from the fairness of outcomes or of procedures) and he is likely to feel and react less negatively now. This is interactional fairness, consisting of informational fairness and interpersonal fairness.

The above-outlined aspects you realized from the Exercise 1 are described in greater detail as a part of this chapter.

What is justice?

The term "justice" can be understood from its relation to the word "just." The synonyms for the word "just" are fair, objective, even-handed, unbiased. These synonyms also imply other possible meanings of just as due or deserved, suggesting that an outcome or treatment received by an individual is viewed as just by the individual when it gives him/her what is due to or deserved by him/her. Justice is facilitated by the objective evaluation of facts and morally appropriate evaluation of facts (Locke, 2003). An individual is likely to receive what he/she deserves or what is due to him/her when the decision-making process associated with that outcome or treatment allocation is objective and unbiased. Objectivity and lack of bias suggests that the relevant facts of the person's circumstances were considered and the facts were evaluated in a morally sound manner by avoiding any bias against the individual. Such inclusion of all facts and morally sound evaluation will provide the individual a fair or just assessment of his/her contributions and facilitate the individual's receipt of fair or just outcomes. In this sense, objectivity and lack of bias or presence of moral soundness facilitate fairness or justice.

Why are justice considerations involved in human life?

In general human life, no single individual is completely capable of fulfilling all his/her needs single-handedly. An individual works on a job, gets an income out of it, and uses his/her income to purchase things such as accommodation on rent, food, clothing, and transport to fulfill his/her needs such as shelter, nourishment, and mobility. Many of such exchange transactions are likely to work reasonably satisfactorily if there is some element of trust between the transacting individuals. For example, an individual with money will need to trust the food vendor to some extent to believe that the food sold to him/her will provide him/her reasonable benefits for the money and that the food will indeed be provided to him/her after paying the money. This trust will be formed and sustained when the food vendor pursues his/her self-interests of obtaining the food-seeking individual's cash only in return for the actual or promised provision of an appropriate amount of food. The trust will not be formed if the food vendor pursues his/her self-interest of obtaining the food-seeking individual's cash by taking the cash but not actually delivering the appropriate quantity or right quality of food or, at an extreme, by forcibly snatching the cash from the food-seeking individual. Thus, in a general sense, trust and cooperation between two parties will be formed and sustained when each party restrains from pursuing its self-interests in such a way as to not hurt the other party's self-interests.

In this way, justice represents a moral norm of self-restraint in one's pursuit of self-interests to ensure that pursuing one's self-interests does not harm another's self-interests. Through this balancing of self-interests of various parties in a collective effort such as exchange or collective productive activity, justice facilitates trust and cooperation in human groups and societies. Justice, in general in human life, reflects the conditions of fairness or justness in a human group or society, indicating that others will pursue their self-interests in a fair or just manner that ensures that one's own self-interests will also be justly or fairly honored or protected. Thus, justice is an important and required feature of human groups or society because without it cooperative collective action may not be sustained. This importance of justice in human life is reflected in various expressions in the literature. One expression states, "In all people, without exception, there lives some instinct for truth, some attraction toward justice" (Franklin D. Roosevelt quoted in Sashkin and Williams [1990, p. 56]). Another expression states, "Justice, sir, is the greatest interest of man on earth" (Daniel Webster quoted in Cropanzano, Bowen, and Gilliland [2007, p. 34]). Both of these expressions indicate the likely importance of justice for human beings in general.

What is organizational justice?

While justice, as indicated in the preceding discussion, matters in general human life, it also matters for employees in the specific context of work organizations. Employees' perceptions or assessment of fairness in organizations is referred to as "organizational justice." Organizational justice reflects employee perceptions of the moral appropriateness of the organizations' actions towards them. As organizational actions are executed by managers, organizational justice reflects employees' assessment of the moral appropriateness of managerial actions in an organization (Cropanzano et al., 2007, p. 35).

Organizational justice perceptions of employees are likely to be based on several decisions of distributing to them various outcomes such as incentives, pay raises, promotions, training opportunities, challenging or interesting job assignments, warnings, pay deduction, pay reduction, punitive actions, and layoffs. In considering an organization's decision-making for the distribution of such outcomes, employees also consider the way decision makers or the organization has treated them. Thus, employee perceptions of organizational justice consider not only the fairness of outcomes but also the moral appropriateness of the treatment received from an organization or managers in an organization. Thus, organizational justice takes many forms covering the outcome and treatment aspects.

Forms of organizational justice

Sashkin and Williams (1990) compared, within a single organization, five stores having high employee sickness and accidents compensation costs with five stores having low costs and found that the low cost stores, in general, had higher justice climate than high cost stores. This may suggest that justice climate benefits both employee well-being and the organization. Further, a review of empirical research using meta-analysis found that organizational justice climate of a work unit such as a team, branch, and organization has a positive association with work unit effectiveness (Whitman, Caleo, Carpenter, Horner, and Bernerth, 2012, p. 782–783). While this indicates the significance of overall justice for organizations and managers, there are multiple forms of organizational justice. Fairness of outcomes is referred to as distributive justice (e.g., Folger and Konovsky, 1989, p. 115) while fairness of procedures is referred to as procedural justice and fairness of treatment is referred to as interactional justice (e.g., Masterson, Lewis, Goldman, and Taylor, 2000, p. 739). Thus, three forms of organizational justice are distributive justice, procedural justice, and interactional justice. Each of these three forms of justice is described below. Employee-related outcomes and why different justice forms result in these outcomes are also outlined below. Prior to the detailed description, an integrated overview, summarizing the description provided in the following parts of this chapter, of various forms of justice, their employee-related outcomes, and the processes through which these outcomes are likely to occur is depicted in Figure 6.1.

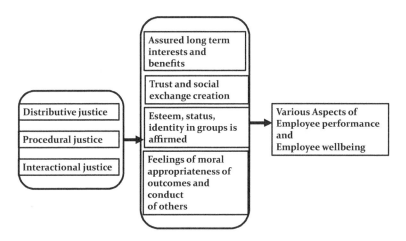

Figure 6.1 What effects justice has and why?

Source: Partly based on various works including Cropanzano, et al. (2001, p. 176), Cropanzano et al. (2007), Konovsky (2000), and Moorman and Byrne (2005) and on a summary of the detailed description in the following parts of this chapter.

Distributive justice

What is distributive justice?

Distributive justice is the term used to refer to employee judgments of the fairness in the distribution of outcomes to them. Outcomes include not only the monetary rewards such as pay raise but also various other positive outcomes such as training opportunities, other benefits, promotions, and challenging or interesting job assignments. Equity theory of Adams (1965) is the main framework for examining distributive justice (Greenberg, 2009).

Equity theory (Adams, 1965) suggests the following. An employee prefers equity, which is a state in which the employee's ratio of outcomes to inputs is regarded as fair. This state, referred to as equity, is satisfactory for an employee. While outcomes refer to various positive outcomes such as pay, training program nominations, interesting job assignments, and benefits received by an employee, inputs refer to various contributions of an employee to an organization and may include employee education, experience, hours worked, and risks taken for doing the work in the organization. An employee strives to maintain equity. For assessing equity or fairness of one's outcome-input ratio, an employee compares his/her outcome-input ratio to that of a "referent" other. The referent other is an individual with whose outcome-input ratio the employee chooses to compare his/her own outcome-input ratio. This referent chosen for the comparison by an employee could be some similar employee such as a coworker doing a similar job or a coworker with a similar education and experience level.

Equity theory (e.g., Adams, 1965) also suggests the following. While the equality of an employee's outcome-input ratio with the outcome-input ratio of the referent is satisfactory to the employee, two kinds of inequalities that, in principle, can occur are not satisfying. The first form of inequality is underreward inequity, in which the outcome-input ratio of an employee is smaller than that of the referent. The affective reaction of an employee to the underreward inequity is that of resentment. The second form of inequality is orverreward inequity, in which the outcome-input ratio of an employee is larger than that of the referent. The affective reaction of an employee to the overreward inequity is overreward guilt. Both forms of inequities – underreward inequity and overreward inequity – are dissatisfying to an individual experiencing them.

Equity theory (Adams, 1963, p. 427) further suggests that when an employee is in the state of inequity, he/she will attempt to restore equity. For restoring equity, there are several responses an employee can make in the state of inequity. Various possible responses, based on equity theory (1963; Adams, 1965), of an employee to restore equity from the state of inequity are illustrated below with an example. As a hypothetical example, consider the following table. In this table, outcome-to-input ratio is based on certain units of outcomes and inputs. The outcomes and inputs are both reduced to common units. For this, all inputs such as the education level, experience, and effort level of an employee are converted into a common unit, and similar conversion is done for various outcomes such as pay level, other benefits, training opportunities, and interesting assignments. Thus, through such mental work of an employee, he/she can arrive at his/her own outcome-to-input ratio in his/her organization.

Outcome/ Input Ratio for Self (An Employee)	Outcome/Input Ratio for Referent (e.g., Employee's Coworker)	Equity or Inequity State	Feeling (of the Employee)
20/10 = 2	16/8 = 2	Equity	Satisfaction
20/10 = 2	16/4 = 4	Underreward Inequity	Underreward Resentment
20/10 = 2	16/10 = 1.6	Overreward Inequity	Overreward Guilt

In the above hypothetical example, in the situation in the first row where the outcome-to-input ratio of an employee is equal to that of the referent, the resulting state is that of equity which is satisfying and hence this state will not induce the employee to take any actions to restore equity because equity already exists. Now, let us consider the second situation in the second row where the outcome-to-input ratio of the self (an employee) is two and that of the referent is four and the resulting state for the employee is that of underreward and the associated feelings of anger or resentment. In this state of inequity, the employee will seek to restore equity for which there are, according to equity theory (e.g., Adams, 1965), multiple possible options.

First, the employee could, according to equity theory (e.g., Adams, 1963, p. 427, 428), change his/her own inputs or outcomes. For example, he/she could reduce his/her inputs by putting in less effort and bringing his/her inputs from ten units to five units so that his/her now revised outcome-to-input ratio becomes 4 (20 divided by 5 = 4), which is equal to the referent and hence the equity gets restored for the employee. In an actual organizational context, the reduction of effort by an employee could take various forms such as working slow, remaining absent on a heavy work day, avoiding difficult task assignments, or lowering one's extra positive contributions such as organizational citizenship behaviors. As another response, the employee could try to increase his/her outcomes without increasing his/her inputs. For example, he/she could increase his/her outcomes from 20 units to 40 units so that his/her now revised outcome-to-input ratio becomes four which is equal to the ratio of referent and hence equity is restored. In an actual organizational context, an employee may steal the organization's property or engage in politics to increase his/her outcomes without increasing his/her inputs on the job. Indeed, the research indicates that theft is a response which individuals make in responding to underreward inequity (e.g., Greenberg, 1990; 1993).

Second, an employee, in the state of underreward inequity, could also, according to equity theory (e.g., Adams, 1963, p. 429), change the inputs of the referent coworker. For example, the employee could increase the inputs of the referent to eight units from the current four units so that the outcome-to-input ratio of the referent becomes 2, which is equal to that of the employee and hence the equity gets restored. In an actual organizational context, an employee could increase the inputs of the referent coworker through various actions such as shifting risky or difficult tasks to the referent coworker, by hiding his/her raw materials, or by breaking down his/her machine and making the work more difficult and effort-consuming. Further, in the state of inequity, an employee can also reduce the outcomes of the referent from 16 units to eight units so that the revised outcome-to-input ratio of the referent becomes 2, which is equal to that of the employee and hence the equity is restored. In an actual organizational context, an employee could decrease the outcomes of the referent coworker through various actions such as spreading negative rumors about his/her performance and hence lowering his/her performance appraisals and lodging false complaints about the performance levels of the referent coworker.

Third, an employee, in the state of underreward inequity, can also, according to equity theory (e.g., Adams, 1963, p. 428), cognitively change his/her inputs and/or outcomes or his/her referent coworker's inputs and/or outcomes. For example, an employee could deliberately distort his/her perceptions to misbelieve that he/she puts in less effort or receives certain outcomes which are more valued or the referent coworker's job requires more effort or certain outcomes of the referent coworker are not valuable. Such perceptual or cognitive (mental) distortions may help the employee to increase his/her outcome-input ratio or reduce the outcome-to-input ratio of the referent coworker and bring the revised ratio closer to his/her own outcome-to-input ratio and thereby partly or completely remove the underreward inequity experienced by the employee.

Finally, in addition to the above outlined three actions, an employee experiencing underreward inequity could also, according to equity theory (e.g., Adams, 1963, p. 428), change the referent or leave the field. In case of the action of changing the referent, an employee experiencing underreward inequity may replace his/her current referent coworker with a coworker who has an outcome-to-input ratio closer to his/her own outcome-to-input ratio and thereby partly or completely remove the underreward inequity experienced by him/her. In case of the action of leaving the field, an employee experiencing underreward inequity may seek a transfer to another work unit or department or leave the organization so that he/she can avoid being in the situation of underreward inequity.

In the above description, the situation from the second row of the table forming underreward inequity was used in order to facilitate the description of various actions an employee could take to restore equity from the state of underreward inequity. A similar pattern of responses for restoring equity also occurs, as per equity theory (Adams, 1965), in the situation of overreward inequity. The responses of changing the referent and leaving the field can be used to restore equity by an employee experiencing overreward inequity. In case an employee adopts the options of changing or cognitively distorting the outcomes or inputs of his/her own or the referent, the direction of these changes would be such as to partly or completely remove the overreward inequity. For example, an employee, in the state of overreward inequity, is likely to reduce his/her outcomes or increase his/her inputs (e.g., put in extra effort on the job) in order to partly or completely remove the overreward inequity and overreward guilt experienced by him/her.

Though it may be difficult to believe that an individual would make responses in order to remove the state of overreward inequity in order to attain the state of equity, research findings indicate that such responses occur. For example, consider a hypothetical situation involving a research study in which students with similar age and education level are brought in as participants (subjects) in an experiment. In the experiment, the students are assigned to two groups. Each group is required to do, for the duration of about an hour, a simple task such as coding questionnaires. While doing the task, one group is provided the perception that it is overpaid. The group perceiving overreward inequity puts in more effort through actions such as delivering more quantity or reducing errors which in that situation is believed to be instrumental in reducing the overreward inequity (e.g., Goodman and Friedman, 1969, p. 368–371). These responses reflect the overreward inequity group's attempts to increase its effort (i.e., inputs) in order to partly or completely remove the overreward inequity and to approach equity. It may be noted that in research study situations, the students in the overpaid group cannot cognitively distort their inputs or the outcomes of the other group because in this laboratory situation all outcomes other than the payment are likely to be almost similar in both the groups. With such exclusion of multiple cognitive distortion possibilities, the higher paid group cannot use the cognitive distortion option to remove their overreward inequity. Thus, experiencing overreward inequity, the higher paid group seeks to increase its inputs or effort through actions that are seen as instrumental in reducing the overreward inequity.

Why do employees pay attention to distributive justice?

Human beings have a tendency to consider what they receive with what they expect to receive from their exchange processes, and the expectation is likely to be based on the comparisons with other situations or groups (e.g., Adams, 1963, p. 424). For a person to determine what he/she expects to receive, he/she may do a comparison with what other socially comparable individuals receive. When what is received by a person is short of what he/she expects to receive, a sense of relative deprivation and the resulting feelings of injustice and resentment can develop (e.g., Greenberg, 1987. p. 11–12). For example, consider primary school and high school students. When assessed answer scripts of an examination or test, with marks of students written on them, are returned to students in a classroom, it is likely that a student looks at his/her own scores and then inquires of the student sitting next to him/her as to how many marks he/she received. This is a process of social comparison. If a student who believes he/she is more knowledgeable and had studied much harder for the test than his/her neighboring student and receives a lower score than the neighboring student, then he/she is likely to feel that his/her scores are unfair and is likely to experience underreward inequity. As another example, consider a family with two children with only a couple of years of difference in their age. It is likely that, at the breakfast table, a child is quite happy with the items served to him/her at breakfast. However, the moment he/she sees that his/her brother or sister has more or better items on his/her plate, this child is likely to feel upset as a reflection of his/her feeling of underreward inequity coming from the child's doing comparison with his/her brother or sister.

As described in the above examples, and as outlined in various theories of responses to outcome distribution (e.g. Greenberg, 1987, p. 11–12), the judgments of distributive justice possibly emerge because of the social comparison tendency of human beings. The social comparison process sets the expectation level of an individual. When the actual receipt of outcomes is less than the expected outcome, a sense of relative deprivation and the resulting feelings of distributive injustice can come (e.g. Greenberg, 1987, p. 11–12). This suggests that judgments of distributive justice are likely to be part of an employee's work in an organization where he/she potentially expects and receives outcomes.

Likely consequences of distributive justice (and injustice)

Research findings indicate several consequences of distributive injustice. As described in the preceding part, distributive injustice or underreward inequity experienced by an employee can result in the employee's engaging in acts of theft (e.g., Greenberg, 1990). The affective response coming from underreward inequity or failure of distributive justice is that of underreward resentment or anger. In the emotional space or circumplex, anger forms a part of negative emotions (e.g., Daniels, 2000). Emotional or subjective well-being is the net of positive emotions over negative emotions (Daniels, 2000; Keyes, Shmotkin, and Ryff, 2002). Thus, occurrence of the negative emotion of anger in response to distributive injustice implies that distributive injustice is likely to lower the emotional well-being of employees. Further, there is a positive association of distributive justice with job satisfaction (Cohen-Charash and Spector, 2001; Colquitt et al., 2001). Job satisfaction is an important work attitude of employees. It is positively associated with some positive outcomes such as employees' task performance (Judge, Thoresen, Bono, and Patton, 2001) and contextual performance or organizational citizenship behaviors (e.g., Podsakoff, MacKenzie, Paine, and Bacharach, 2000). Thus, distributive injustice in an organization is likely to lower the job satisfaction of employees and is also likely to lower employees' task performance and contextual performance. This is consistent with research findings that there is a positive association between distributive justice and employees' task performance and contextual performance (Cohen-Charash and Spector, 2001; Colquitt et al., 2001). Further, distributive justice is also negatively correlated with employees' counterproductive work behavior (Cohen-Charash and

Spector, 2001) and negative reactions (Colquitt et al., 2001). Results contained in several meta-analytic reviews – reviews which quantitatively aggregate and average results from several empirical research studies – provide findings similar to those outlined above on the outcomes of distributive justice. A meta-analytic review (Viswesvaran and Ones, 2002, p. 199) contains results which provide a support for a positive relationship between distributive justice and employees' productivity, organizational citizenship behaviors, and job satisfaction. Some of the meta-analytic review results in Lee and Cropanzano (2009, p. 797) indicate a positive relationship of distributive justice with employees' job satisfaction in both North American and East Asian contexts. Some of the results reported in a recent meta-analytic review (Colquitt, Scott, Rodell, Long, Zapata, Colon, D. E., and Wesson, 2013, p. 207–9, 218) indicate that distributive justice has a positive association with employees' task performance, organizational citizenship behaviors and positive affect, and a negative relationship with counterproductive behaviors at work and negative affect. From some of the correlations reported in the results of meta-analysis-based review by Rupp, Shao, Jones, and Liao (2014, p. 168–169), it can be inferred that distributive justice has a positive association with employees' organizational citizenship behaviors and job satisfaction and a negative association with counterproductive behaviors at work.

How can distributive justice be enhanced?

Distributive justice can be enhanced by enhancing the equality of outcome-input ratios of employees in an organization. Various human resource management activities can facilitate this. For example, providing a pay raise based on performance and thus facilitating a link between the effort put in by employees (input) and pay raise outcome will enhance the equality of outcome-input ratios for employees doing similar jobs. Distributive justice across job levels can be enhanced by using appropriate methods of job evaluation so that the pay levels for different jobs reflect the extent and nature of inputs required by the different jobs. Within a job type or job family, providing different levels of salary to candidates based on their different levels of educational qualifications and experience will also enhance the possibility of having an equal outcome-input ratio for employees within a job type or job family.

The above inputs describe some of the usual human resource management actions. Some examples of unusual or innovative human resource management actions are described below.

In a bank, a certain category of clerical staff did not have the authority to clear checks, and hence checks had to go through the time-consuming process of obtaining the clearance of officers with a higher level of authority. So, in order to shorten the check-processing time, the top management decided to provide the clerical staff the authority to clear checks below a certain amount. However, some clerical staff seemed reluctant to accept this additional responsibility, which would create additional work for them. The top management then announced a scheme in which the clerical staff accepting this additional authority and task were to be provided an additional monthly pay of certain amount. This worked. In this example, providing additional pay increased the clerical staff's outcomes and thus compensated for their additional inputs (taking on additional responsibility and an additional task) thus maintaining the equality of their new outcome-input ratios with their own earlier outcome-input ratio and also the equality of their new outcome-input ratio and with clerical staff who did not accept this additional responsibility.

Consider another example in a bank, staff posted at certain locations in inadequately developed areas were provided additional allowances/benefits. In this example, the hardships suffered at such locations represent additional inputs put in by the employees posted in those locations. Providing additional allowances/benefits for those extra inputs means giving additional outcomes for additional inputs and thus can facilitate maintaining the equality of outcome-input ratio of these employees with the other employees who are not transferred to such inadequately developed locations.

Consider one more example in a bank, new recruits are required to take certain internal assessment examinations toward the end of their initial training period, which includes in-class training and on-the-job training. Among those who pass this examination, those who perform very well in the examination are confirmed in a higher position/level than those who perform only moderately well in the examination. In this example, those who perform very well in the examination are likely to have higher intelligence, are likely to have worked harder during the training program to learn the training inputs, and are also likely to have more knowledge than those who did not perform very well in the examination. Thus, their inputs into the organization are higher than those not performing very well in the examination. Providing a higher position/level to the employees performing very well in the examination adds to their outcomes from the organization. This is because the higher level of position carries, in principle, greater authority and prestige and is also likely to carry a higher pay level. Thus, the outcome-input ratio of the employees performing very well in the examination is likely to go closer to being equal to the outcome-input ratio of the employees who did not perform very well.

Procedural justice

What is procedural justice?

Procedural justice refers to the extent of fairness in the procedures used for making decisions (e.g., Masterson et al., 2000, p. 739). This fairness assessment focuses on procedures and is separate from the assessment of the fairness of the outcomes that employees receive from the use of procedures.

Early research on the legal proceedings in courts examined the effects of providing litigants greater control over presenting – selecting and developing – evidence and such control was referred to as "process control" (e.g., Greenberg, 1987, p. 14). This research found that when a party to a litigation has control over selecting and developing evidence, the verdict is likely to be perceived as more fair and likely to be better accepted by the party than when the party has no control over selecting and developing evidence (Greenberg, 1987, p. 14). Further, it was found that when litigants had voice – a say in the decision-making procedures – they expressed enhanced acceptance of unfavorable verdicts (Greenberg, 1987, p. 14).

While the early research examined procedural justice in terms of "process control," the subsequent research identified the features of procedures that employees consider in assessing procedural justice. These features of procedures described in the literature come from two works (Leventhal, 1980 and Leventhal, Karuza, and/or Fry, 1980, as cited in various works such Greenberg, 1987, p. 14–15; Masterson et al., 2000, p. 730, Moorman, 1991, p. 847). Ethicality in terms of adherence of procedures with the ethical and moral standards of the individuals involved, accuracy, consistency, bias suppression, correctibility, identification of decision-making power, providing opportunities to select decision makers, scope for making changes in procedures (Greenberg, 1987, p. 15), and also taking into account the values and concerns (Greenberg, 2009, p. 257) of individuals affected by the decisions are among the features of procedures that individuals consider in assessing the extent of procedural fairness. Such characteristics of fair procedures suggested by researchers have evolved from the work of Leventhal, Karuza, and Fry (1980, as cited in Colquitt, 2001, p. 388; Greenberg, 1987, pp. 14–15). Each of these features mentioned in and based on the above cited literature is described below.

Ethicality refers to the extent to which the procedures are based on the prevalent moral and ethical standards (e.g., Greenberg, 1987, p. 15). For example, the procedures that use only oral and not written evidence may not be ethical, as they unreasonably exclude the consideration of relevant evidence. As another example, procedures that punish salespersons for not making false promises about the products to customers is likely to be lacking the ethicality features, as it is not in line with the moral value of honesty.

Accuracy of the information used in making decisions about outcomes is another feature Greenberg (1987, p. 15) that determines the extent of procedural justice. For example, in determining the penalty for employee late arrival, the lateness assessed from the time of arrival recorded by a properly functioning clock is likely to provide greater accuracy than the lateness assessed by the supervisors' subjective perceptions of employees' lateness. Thus, use of a properly functioning clock rather than the supervisor's subjective judgment for determining the extent of lateness of an employee for determining the punitive action for lateness is likely to enhance procedural justice perceptions of employees.

Consistency refers to the extent to which the same procedures are applied to all employees in similar situations (e.g., Greenberg, 2009). For example, if the norm of condoning less than five minutes of lateness is applied to only some and not all employees, such a procedure will have low consistency and hence employees are likely to perceive low procedural justice.

The bias suppression feature requires that a decision maker's self-interests or subjective preconception do not influence the procedures (Greenberg, 2009). For example, freedom from subjective preconceptions would mean that the procedures do not have the potential to adversely affect one or some group, such as women, old employees, or an employee from a particular region, race, department, function, etc. For example, if the preconception that employees who take long leave are not committed to work or that women employees are not efficient is reflected in organizational procedures, the procedures may consider taking leave for more than two weeks at a stretch as a lapse and provide punitive outcomes for taking leave for more than two weeks. Such procedures then are likely to affect women who may require a long duration of maternity leave. In this example, such procedures may have come about because of either the decision maker's preconceptions about women or the self-interests of the male-dominated group of decision makers who wish to maintain their dominance in organizational decisions. The net result of such procedures is that there is bias against a group of individuals and procedures reflect the potential for a particular form of allocation or decision, namely decisions that are likely to provide more punitive outcomes to women than to men.

Correctibility, as a feature of fair procedures, refers to the provision of a mechanism in the procedures for correcting the incorrect decisions. Thus, correctibility implies the presence of an appeal mechanism in which appeals can be heard (Greenberg, 1987) and also the utility of the appeal mechanism for correcting the incorrect decisions (Greenberg, 2009). For example, if procedures allow an employee to appeal against what he/she perceives to be an unfavorable decision and the appeal process is such that a genuinely incorrect decision is rectified and the correct decision is made based on the employee appeal, the employees are likely to perceive a higher level of procedural justice. Consider an employee who has received a less than fair annual pay increase. If he/she can appeal to the human resource management department or some authority in the organization for reviewing his/her annual pay raise and providing the fair amount of annual pay raise and if there is a reasonable possibility that the appeal process will do the required rectification and grant the revised fair amount of pay raise to the employee, then the procedure will have the correctibility feature and provide high procedural justice.

Identification of decision-making power (Greenberg, 1987, p. 15) seems to refer to the extent of information shared with the employees about the individuals involved in making decisions about employees and their decision-making powers. For example, if procedures clearly describe who is authorized to record and evaluate the evidence and make the decision about employees, then employees are likely to perceive high procedural fairness in these procedures.

Procedures which provide employees an opportunity to select decision makers and scope for revising procedures (Greenberg, 1987, p. 15) are likely to be perceived as fair by the employees. For example, if the committee that makes employee job allocation decisions or training program nomination decisions is constituted of members identified by the employees, then employees are likely to view the procedures as fair. Similarly, if employees can suggest and cause revisions in the procedures, the procedures are likely to be viewed as fair.

Representing the values and concerns of employees in the procedures is another aspect of procedural fairness (e.g., Greenberg, 2009, p. 257). This aspect may be incorporated by providing employees participation in the design and implementation of the procedures, as this may provide scope for the inclusion of employees' concerns and outlooks in the procedures. For example, in designing procedures to decide on employee-related matters, if employees are provided participation in the decision-making process, employees may be able to express their concerns, views, and needs and there is likely to be some scope for their incorporation into the procedures.

The above description suggests that employees consider various features of procedures, covered in the literature (e.g., Colquitt, 2001; Greenberg, 1987; Greenberg, 2009), in order to form perceptions of procedural fairness. Managers and students, when asked about which features of procedures enhance procedural fairness, mention some features other than those described above from the literature. Transparency of procedures is one such feature. Some managers and students feel that when procedures are transparent to the employees, then employees are likely to view procedures as more fair. Speed or timeliness of decision making is another feature which gets sometimes mentioned by managers and students as potentially contributing to procedural fairness. These and other features may enhance employee perceptions of fair procedures, because empirical findings in Colquitt et al. (2001) indicate that when several of the procedural features from literature are taken together, they collectively explain only a part of employee perceptions of procedural fairness.

Why do employees pay attention to procedural justice?

Employees pay attention to procedural justice for several reasons. First, the presence of procedural justice conveys to the employees that their self-interests or long term benefits are protected in the long term (e.g., Cropanzano et al., 2007; Folger and Konovsky, 1989; Konovsky, 2000). Thus, when the procedural justice level in an organization is high, employees feel reassured that they would receive their due gains from their organization in the long term. For example, if the procedures used to determine employee pay raise in an organization have the features such as accuracy of information used and correctibility, these features will convey to employees that they will receive appropriate or deserved amounts of pay raises in the organization. Thus, fair procedures have some amount of utilitarian value to employees, as they signal to employees that they will receive their fair outcomes in the long term.

Second, procedural justice provision by an organization induces employees to develop trust in the organization (Konovsky and Pugh, 1994; Moorman and Byrne, 2005). Trust between two parties facilitates the development of social exchange between the parties (e.g., Konovsky, 2000). Social exchange is different from economic exchange between two parties. In an economic exchange, the items to be exchanged, the timeline for their exchange, etc. are specified, whereas in a social exchange, the exchange of items is not one for one and not necessarily immediate (e.g., Konovsky, 2000). Thus, employees are likely to be concerned about procedural justice provision from an organization for deciding whether to trust the organization and whether to form a social exchange relationship with the organization.

Third, when procedural justice level in an organization is high, the procedures are likely to have the features such as consistency, bias suppression, and correctibility. These features are likely to convey to the employees in that organization that the organization, through the adoption of such procedural features, honors their sense of self-respect and dignity (e.g., Folger and Konovsky, 1989, p. 126) and that the organization respects the employees (Moorman and Byrne, 2005, p. 369). As employees, as human beings, are likely to want their sense of self-respect and dignity upheld by others, they are likely to seek procedural justice to preserve and enhance their sense of self-respect and dignity. Thus, fair procedures can serve as a signal, message, or symbol that the organization honors employees' self-respect and dignity. In this sense, procedural fairness has nonmaterial value or social value for employees.

Fourth, procedural justice can convey to employees the moral appropriateness of managerial conduct. Procedural justice implies that the procedures used are consistent with prevailing moral values and are free from bias (e.g., Greenberg, 2009). Thus, when procedural justice is present, employees are likely to infer that the managers who used the procedures have engaged in morally appropriate conduct by using fair procedures for making the decisions. Thus, the presence of procedural justice implies moral appropriateness of managerial actions. In this sense, employees are likely to value fair procedures, as they allow employees to feel assured that the managerial conduct, when governed by fair procedures, is morally sound.

The above discussion, which is based on the literature (e.g., Folger and Konovsky, 1989; Cropanzano at al., 2007; Greenberg, 2009; Konovsky, 2000; Konovsky and Pugh, 1994; Moorman and Byrne, 2005) and partly summarized in Figure 6.1, suggests that procedural justice provision by an organization is likely to matter for various reasons summarized below in an organization. Procedural justice in an organization matters for employees because it signals to them the likelihood of receiving their short-term and long-term due benefits. Further, procedural justice can encourage employees to trust an organization and develop a social exchange relationship with the organization. Procedural justice from an organization matters for employees also because it helps them infer the organization's concern for their self-respect and dignity. Finally, procedural justice helps employees to infer the moral appropriateness of managerial conduct. Thus, employees are likely to pay attention to procedural justice in an organization for both material reasons and also for nonmaterial reasons. These multiple reasons for why employees pay attention to procedural justice reflect, to some extent, the various utilitarian, esteem- and acceptance-seeking in relations, and moral values or meaning-related considerations concerning the significance of organizational justice, in general, noted in research (e.g., Cropanzano et al., 2001, P. 176).

Likely consequences of procedural justice (and injustice)

Procedural justice can influence various performance-related and well-being-related outcomes of employees as outlined below. Procedural justice influences employees' job satisfaction (e.g., Folger and Konovsky, 1989). Procedural justice is positively associated with employees' intrinsic satisfaction and extrinsic satisfaction (Cohen-Charash and Spector, 2001) and with job satisfaction (Colquitt et al., 2001). Procedural justice is also positively associated with employees' satisfaction with the supervisor and management (Cohen-Charash and Spector, 2001). Thus, procedural justice is associated with multiple forms of employees' satisfaction in an organization. A recent study (Cassar and Buttigieg, 2015, p. 225–226) reported a positive relationship of procedural justice with employees' emotional well-being.

Positive association between procedural justice and employee trust is also noted in Colquitt et al. (2001). Procedural justice is positively associated with employees' task performance (e.g., Cohen-Charash and Spector, 2001; Colquitt et al., 2001). Procedural justice is positively associated with employees' organizational citizenship behaviors (Cohen-Charash and Spector, 2001; Colquitt et al., 2001). Procedural justice is negatively associated with employees' counterproductive behaviors (Cohen-Charash and Spector, 2001), which are a form of employees' negative behaviors.

Results contained in several meta-analytic reviews provide findings similar to those outlined above on the employee performance and well-being outcomes of procedural justice. A meta-analytic review (Viswesvaran and Ones, 2002, p. 199) contains results which provide a support for a positive relationship between procedural justice and employees' productivity, organizational citizenship behaviors, and job satisfaction. Some of the results reported in the meta-analytic review by Skitka, Winquist, and Hutchinson (2003, p. 326–327) indicate that procedural fairness has a positive relationship with employee task performance, organizational citizenship behavior, and task satisfaction and a negative relationship with negative emotions and retaliation form of negative behaviors. Some of the meta-analytic review results in Lee and Cropanzano (2009, p. 797) indicate a positive relationship of procedural justice with employees' job satisfaction in both North American and East Asian contexts. Some of the results reported in a recent meta-analytic review (Colquitt et al., 2013, p. 207–9, 218) indicate that procedural justice has a positive association with employees' task performance, organizational citizenship behaviors and positive affect, and a negative relationship with counterproductive behaviors at work and negative affect. From some of the correlations reported in the results of meta-analysis-based review by Rupp et al. (2014, p. 168–169), it can be inferred that procedural justice has a positive association with employees' organizational citizenship behaviors and job satisfaction and a negative association with counterproductive behaviors at work.

The above discussion suggests that when employees experience procedural justice, they are likely to have higher satisfaction with the job, have high emotional well-being, trust in the supervisor and organization, perform better on the task, perform organizational citizenship behaviors, and refrain from performing negative behaviors.

The above discussion outlined several likely positive consequences of procedural justice. Now, consider the other form of justice described earlier, namely distributive justice. When employees do not receive distributive justice, the resulting experience is that of distributive injustice. When employees experience distributive injustice, employees have negative responses, as outlined earlier, such as a drop in satisfaction and the performance of negative behaviors. Procedural justice can lower the extent of employees' such negative reactions coming from distributive injustice. For example, when individuals engage in stealing as a response to distributive injustice, the presence of procedural justice lowers amount of stealing the individuals engage in (Greenberg, 1993). As another example, the presence of procedural justice lowers the drop in the job satisfaction of those employees who have experienced distributive injustice (McFarlin and Sweeney, 1992).

Overall, procedural justice has positive effects on employees' positive behaviors, including employee performance, and employees' job satisfaction. In addition, while distributive injustice induces negative employee reactions such as stealing and a drop in job satisfaction, procedural justice can weaken such negative reactions to distributive injustice. Thus, procedural justice can create positive effects on employees' performance and well-being and can also act as a protective shield against employees' negative reactions to distributive injustice.

How can procedural justice be enhanced?

Employee perceptions of procedural justice are influenced by several features of procedures. As described earlier, these features of procedures include adherence of procedures with the prevalent moral and ethical norms, identification of decision-making power, making procedures represent employees' concerns and views, using procedures based on accurate information, applying procedures consistently across employees, keeping procedures free from bias, and including scope in procedures for correcting inappropriate decisions (e.g., Greenberg, 1987; Greenberg, 2009). Enhancing the extent of these features in the procedures is likely to increase the level of procedural justice perceived by employees. Some examples of the possible actions for enhancing employee perceptions of procedural justice by enhancing the extent of these features in the procedures are outlined below.

The ethicality feature refers to the extent to which procedures reflect the relevant ethical and moral standards (e.g., Greenberg, 1987, p. 15). A general ethical norm is that judgments should be made based on objective evidence and not on subjective impressions. Consider the situation of forming a judgment about an employee's compliance with the work procedures. Requiring employees to comply with work procedures dictated by their supervisors even when the procedures have the potential to cause harm to the employees themselves or to coworkers and then using their compliance or noncompliance as the basis for penalizing them is likely to have low ethicality. This is because requiring employees to expose themselves to harm or to cause harm to others deviates from ethical and moral norms.

The identification of decision-making power feature of procedural justice (Greenberg, 1987) is the extent to which there is clarity about who will make the judgment in deciding employee outcomes and what the powers of these decision makers are. Providing adequately clear information on who will decide which employee-related matters and what their decision-making powers are is likely to enhance this feature of procedure and facilitate employee perceptions of procedural justice. For example, in some academic institutes, in describing the procedure for deciding faculty promotion, a clear description is provided of who will evaluate the information on the performance outcomes of the faculty and who will make the promotion decision. This information is provided in a document titled "faculty manual." Usually, the overall head of the institute carrying the position title of "Director" and one or more of the Deans are likely to be the members of the decision-making authority for faculty promotions. The document is likely to specify the power of this authority for making decisions, such as providing an overall assessment of faculty performance and granting or declining a promotion. Along the same lines, clearly documenting the composition and power of the decision-making authority for various employee-related decisions is likely to enhance the extent of identification of decision-making power feature in the procedures.

This documentation may cover decisions such as confirming employment, transferring employees to different locations, granting annual pay raises to employees, and conferring promotions on employees. The greater the number of decisions for which the decision-making power is documented and the more clarity and sharing of such documented information, the greater is the likelihood of employee perceptions of procedural justice.

Representation or representativeness feature of the procedures (e.g., Greenberg, 2009, p. 257) focuses on the extent to which employees' concerns and views are reflected in the procedures. One possible action to facilitate this is to provide employees some participation in design and implementation of procedures. This will provide scope for making the procedures reflective of employees' views and concerns. If employees are allowed to present the relevant information while decisions are made about them, the representation or representativeness feature in the procedures is likely to be enhanced. For example, in deciding the level of employees' performance and the provision of the consequent rewards to employees, if employees are allowed to prepare a self-appraisal of their performance and submit it to their supervisors, this will provide employees participation in the implementation of the performance assessment and outcome determination process. In an organization whose branch network was spread throughout the country and where transfers were done at multiple locations, the organization had the policy of requiring/allowing employees to indicate a list of a certain number of their preferred locations. This list provided by an employee was considered and an attempt was made to make the transfer of the employee to one of the locations from his/her list of preferred transfer locations. Providing more such participation to employees in implementing decision-making procedures is likely to enhance the "representation" feature in procedures. Such actions are likely to enhance employee perceptions of procedural justice.

Accuracy is the feature of procedures (e.g., Greenberg, 1987) reflecting the extent to which the information used for making decisions is accurate. Accuracy can be seen as freedom from errors. For illustration purpose, consider an example where employee rewards are based on their performance levels during the preceding year. If performance levels are assessed in terms of three categories of low, average, and high based on the judgment of supervisors, the scope for errors is likely to be high and accuracy of the assessed performance level is likely to be low. In contrast, if the performance level of employees is measured on quantitative and accurately count-able indicators such as amount of revenue earned, number of units sold, the number of units produced, etc., then the procedures used for assessing employee performance and providing the consequent rewards to employees is likely to have a high level of accuracy. The resulting high level of accuracy in the procedures is likely to enhance employee perceptions of procedural justice.

Consistency of procedures (e.g., Greenberg, 2009, p. 256) refers to the use of the same procedure for dealing with all employees in similar circumstances and in multiple occurrences of similar instances over a period of time. For example, if only some employ-ees are penalized for late arrival at work and other employees are not penalized, the application of the procedures will not be consist-ent. Hence, employees are likely to perceive low procedural justice. Thus, making procedures applicable to all relevant employees and applying them in a nearly uniform manner can enhance the consist-ency feature and thereby procedural justice.

Bias suppression suggests that procedures are free from inap-propriate preconceptions (e.g., Greenberg, 2009, p. 256) reflects the extent to which the procedures are free from the possibility of causing adverse impact on one group, such as women employees, old employees, or employees belonging to a particular community, region, religion, department, or function. Such adverse impact pos-sibilities could come from incorrect preconceptions or stereotypes such as women not being efficient managers and hence need to be discouraged. Such adverse impact can also come from a decision maker's pursuit of self-interests through procedures. For example, if procedures for providing rewards to employees consider only the amount of extra hours worked, then women and old employees, who are not likely to be in a position to stay back and work extra hours because of their constraints such as other unavoidable and serious family obligations, are likely to suffer an adverse impact. Such procedures may come into play because of the influence of preconceptions about the nonsuitability of women or old employ-ees in the workplace or because of male and young decision makers seeking to pursue their self-interests. Eliminating multiple possibili-ties of such adverse impact on certain groups of employees is likely to enhance the extent of bias suppression feature in procedures and thereby is likely to enhance the level of procedural justice perceived by employees. While it is difficult to anticipate all the likely adverse consequences for all groups, providing employees representation in the judgment-forming process and allowing employees to appeal against adverse decisions and seek correctibility, which are two of the other features of fair procedures, are likely to facilitate identification and rectification of the likely instances of adverse impact for some groups. Revising procedures in order to remove such likely instances is likely to make the procedures more free from the scope for adverse impact on some groups and enhance the extent of bias suppression in the procedures.

Correctibility (e.g., Greenberg, 2009, p. 256) reflects the extent to which the procedures allow the scope for appealing against and rectifying incorrect decisions. Consider a situation of employee performance appraisal and annual pay raise determination. If the procedures clearly specify how and to whom appeals should be made by an employee, in case the employee believes that he/she has received a lower performance appraisal rating than justified by his/her actual performance level and as a result received a lower than deserved annual pay raise, and if the appeal procedures have a reasonable scope for actually rectifying the incorrect decisions, the procedures will have a reasonable degree of correctibility. Employees are likely to experience higher level of procedural justice when such appeal procedures are present. Thus, an organization can enhance employee perceptions of procedural justice by establishing effective appeal procedures and communicating these procedures to employees.

The above description of various features of procedures suggests that an organization will need to identify various important decisions such as making employee transfers, determining annual pay raises, promoting employees, and granting various rewards such as nominations for training programs or provision of high-visibility assignments. For each such decision, an organization will need to ensure that the compliance requirements or standards of accomplishments expected from the employees are not discrepant with the prevalent ethical or moral norms. Further, for each such decision, who will decide and what constitutes the decision maker's decision-making power will need to be clearly specified. Also, employees need to be provided an avenue to provide inputs or their perspective in designing and carrying out the decision-making process. For each decision, it will be necessary to ensure that the information required to make the decision will be available with a high level of accuracy. There will need to be clear guidelines for using procedures consistently across similar situations and for all employees with similar circumstances. An organization will also be required to ensure that compliance requirements or performance standards are such that one group of employees, such as new employees, old employees, senior employees, women employees, or employees with a particular background, are not adversely affected. Further, an organization will also need to establish an appeal process for each of the decisions and clearly communicate it to the employees. Such actions in an organization are likely to enhance the level of procedural justice perceived by employees.

Interactional justice

What is interactional justice?

Interactional justice refers to the fairness of treatment received by employees during the execution of the decision-making procedures (Bies and Moag, 1986 as cited in Masterson, Lewis, Goldman, and Taylor, 2000, p. 739). While this description seems to focus on only the execution of procedures, interactional justice also applies to the process of communication of why procedures were used in a particular manner and why certain decision outcomes were determined (e.g., Colquitt et al., 2001, p. 427). These communications refer to the stage after the decision has been made through the implementation of procedures. When a decision such as a particular level of annual pay increase is communicated to an employee, the treatment provided by the communicating official to the employee during the decision communication also shapes employee perceptions of interactional justice. In light of this part of interactional justice, interactional justice's focus includes not only the treatment provided while implementing the procedures to determine outcomes but also the treatment provided while communicating the decision procedures and outcomes to employees about whom the decisions were made. Individuals expect decisions to be explained to them to an adequate extent and in a respectful manner (Greenberg, 2009). This suggests that interactional justice seems to have two aspects, namely the nature of interpersonal treatment provided and the nature of information provided to employees in implementing procedures and in communicating procedures and decisions. These two aspects are reflected in two components of interactional justice, namely interpersonal justice and informational justice (e.g., Colquitt, 2001, p. 427).

Interpersonal justice refers to the extent to which the interpersonal treatment provided to an employee while executing the procedures and while communicating the procedures and outcomes reflects features such as concern for the sense of self-respect and dignity of the employee (e.g., Cropanzano et al., 2007, p. 39). Interpersonal justice is likely to be experienced by employees when the decision makers are polite, refrain from making improper remarks, and their behaviors convey to the employee that the employee's self-respect and dignity is honored by the decision maker (e.g., Colquitt, 2001; Cropanzano et al., 2007, p. 39).

Informational justice refers to the extent to which the content and process of providing information about procedures and outcomes conveys to the employees that the decision makers have provided adequate justifications for their procedures and decisions and the decision makers have been truthful (e.g., Cropanzano et al., 2007, p. 38). The features of information provision content and process that reflect informational justice include providing comprehensive explanations, providing explanations that are reasonable, being candid while providing information, tailoring the explanations to fit the needs of the employee, and being timely in providing explanations (e.g., Colquitt, 2001).

The above description suggests that employee perceptions of interactional justice are based on two features of the decision maker's behaviors. First, employee perceptions of interactional justice are based on a decision maker's behaviors that are respectful, are polite, and enhance the sense of dignity of the decision recipient. Second, employee perceptions of interactional justice also depend on the nature of information provided to them by the decision makers while executing the decision-making procedures and while communicating the procedures and decisions to the recipients.

Why do employees pay attention to interactional justice?

Human beings have expectations about what is an appropriate manner in which it is fair to treat them. Specifically, people expect that they receive explanations that are adequate and that are provided in a respectful manner (Greenberg, 2009). When a decision maker respectfully provides adequate explanations about procedures and decisions to a recipient, these two features of the decision maker's behaviors are likely to convey to the recipient that they are respected and their sense of dignity is honored. Thus, the recipients are likely to feel that the decision maker's behaviors toward them, as worthy human beings, are "just," because the decision maker behaviors treat them as worthy human beings.

Likely consequences of interactional justice (and injustice)

Interactional justice has a wide range of consequences on various aspects of employee performance and well-being. Some of such consequences of interactional justice are described below based on the empirical evidence available in the existing literature.

Interactional justice has a positive relationship with employees' work performance (Cohen-Charash and Spector, 2001). Interactional justice also has a positive relationship with employees' interpersonal helping behaviors and conscientiousness (Cohen-Charash and Spector, 2001), which are two of the multiple forms of employees' organizational citizenship behaviors. Informational justice, a component of interactional justice, has a positive association with employees' individual-directed and organization-directed organizational citizenship behavior (Colquitt et al., 2001). This suggests that employee experiences of interactional justice may result in employees' higher levels of both task performance and contextual performance or organizational citizenship behaviors.

Interactional justice has a positive relationship with employees' job satisfaction (Cohen-Charash and Spector, 2001; Colquitt et al., 2001) and employees' satisfaction with their supervisors (Cohen-Charash and Spector, 2001). As job satisfaction is a part of employee well-being, the empirically found positive relationship between interactional justice and job satisfaction suggests that employee perceptions of interactional justice can enhance employee well-being. Consistent with this, a recent study (Cassar and Buttigieg, 2015, p. 225–226) reported a positive relationship of interactional justice with employees' emotional well-being.

Both informational justice and interpersonal justice forms of interactional justice have a negative relationship with employees' negative reactions, which are organizationally undesirable behaviors (Colquitt et al., 2001, p. 430, 436). Further, the informational justice component of interactional justice has a negative relationship with employee withdrawal behaviors (Colquitt et al., 2001). Employee withdrawal behaviors can take various forms such as remaining absent, quitting, and neglecting work (e.g., Colquitt et al., 2001, p. 430). A specific form of withdrawal indicator is employees' turnover intention, and interactional justice has a negative relationship with employees' turnover intention (Cohen-Charash and Spector, 2001). Further, some of the results reported in a recent meta-analytic review of empirical research by Colquitt et al, 2013, p. 207–9, 218) indicate that both interpersonal justice and informational justice have a positive association with task performance, organizational citizenship behaviors and positive affect, and a negative relationship with counterproductive behaviors at work and negative affect. Some of the meta-analytic review results in Lee and Cropanzano (2009, p. 797) indicate a positive relationship of interactional justice with employees' job satisfaction in both North American and East Asian contexts. From some of the correlations reported in the results of meta-analysis-based review by Rupp et al. (2014, p. 168–169), it can be inferred that interactional justice has a positive association with employees' organizational citizenship behaviors and job satisfaction and a negative association with counterproductive behaviors at work.

The above description indicates several employee performance-related and well-being-related positive consequences of interactional justice. In addition to these direct consequences, interactional justice can also alleviate employees' negative reactions, such as theft, to distributive injustice. Employees' negative reactions to distributive injustice can be weakened when they experience interactional justice (Greenberg, 1990). Similarly, in an experimental situation, students' theft, as a reaction to distributive injustice, was lower when valid information provision and interpersonal sensitivity aspects of interactional justice were high than when they were low (Greenberg, 1993, p. 94). Further, Greenberg (2006) found that when distributive injustice is present, the negative effects of sleep quality impairment experienced by employees occur, and these negative effects are lowered after the employees' supervisors are trained to provide interactional justice to their subordinates.

In light of interactional justice's positive consequences such as those described above, it is relevant to consider how interactional justice can be enhanced. Some examples of the possible actions for enhancing interactional justice are described below.

How can interactional justice be enhanced?

Interactional justice involves informational justice and interpersonal justice aspects, which require providing adequate and truthful information in a manner which honors a decision-receiving employee's sense of self-respect and dignity (e.g., Cropanzano et al., 2007; Greenberg, 2009). Individual behaviors of a manager that reflect these aspects can enhance employee perceptions of interactional justice. While distributive justice is associated with employee inputs and outcomes, and procedural justice is associated with several features of procedures, interactional justice is focused on a manager's individual behaviors. Therefore, a manager may have greater control over changing the level of interactional justice than changing the level of distributive justice, which might require changing human resource managers' decisions such as certain amounts of reward allocations. Similarly, a manager might have greater control over changing the level of interactional justice than changing the level procedural justice, which might require changing organizational features such as reward determination procedures. Some examples of the possible actions a manager can take to enhance interactional justice through his/her personal behaviors are outlined below.

As an example, consider a decision situation where a manager has to assign a set of jobs among his/her subordinates. Here, a manager can explain the reasons why job assignments are made in a particular way, share with the subordinates information about the criteria that were used to decide about which job is assigned to which subordinate, and ensure that his/her expressions are truthful. Further, a manager can express his/her respect for individual employees through his/her verbal expressions involving the use of polite words and phrases and nonverbal expressions involving gestures, such as offering a seat to his/her subordinates or standing up to receive an employee coming in for a discussion of job assignments. A similar pattern of behaviors could be used by a manager in explaining the procedures and outcomes associated with other organizational decisions such as providing performance rating to subordinates, nominating subordinates for training programs, and requiring employees to stay back beyond office hours to complete extra workload.

As one part of interactional justice – informational justice – involves providing truthful information, in case there is some inadequacy in the procedures such as use information that is not adequately correct, the truthfulness aspect of informational justice would require that the procedural inadequacy be shared with the employee and admitted. Further, the interpersonal justice part of interactional justice requiring the expression of respect for the employee would necessitate that a manager provides apologies (e.g., I am sorry that this happened) or excuses (e.g., it happened accidentally, I had no control over what happened) for the inappropriate aspects of procedures (procedural injustice) or for the unfairness of outcomes (distributive injustice) received by the decision recipient.

Research findings indicate that in cases where employees have experienced distributive injustice employee experience of interactional justice can lower the negative reactions of employees (Greenberg, 1990, 2006). Thus, a manager can pay attention to providing employees interactional justice when other forms of injustice have already occurred. In such situations, a manager's provision of interactional justice can lower employees' negative reactions.

Interactional justice provision actions can have an additional utility. As employee judgments of justice are based on their perceptions, it is likely that employee misperceptions or inadequate information availability to an employee may lead to an employee's misperception that distributive or procedural injustice has occurred. In such situations, while providing interactional justice, a manager can share information on procedures and outcomes to an employee in order to lower the employee's perceptions of procedural and distributive injustice.

For example, when an employee has perceptions of procedural injustice, a manager can explain how procedures used to arrive at the decision had aspects such as consistent application and use of accurate information. A manager can also share information on the available appeal mechanisms. Such information sharing done for providing interactional justice can lower employee misperceptions of procedural justice. Thus, interactional justice provision not only can lower employees' negative reactions to procedural injustice but can also lower employee perceptions of procedural injustice. As another example, when an employee has perceptions of distributive injustice, a manager can explain which inputs of employees were considered in determining the outcomes and how the outcomes received by the employee are fair in light of the inputs provided by the employee. Providing this content while dispensing the informational justice aspect of interactional justice can have three desirable outcomes. First, it can enhance the employee's perception of interactional justice. Second, this content provision while dispensing interactional justice can lower employee perceptions of distributive injustice. Third, this content provision while dispensing interactional justice can also lower the employees' negative reactions to distributive injustice, if distributive injustice continues to be perceived in some magnitude by the employee. Exercise 3 provided at the end of this chapter provides an opportunity to understand the nature of distributive injustice perceived by an employee and to provide interactional justice to an employee in order to attain multiple objectives, such as enhancing employee perceptions of interactional justice, to lower employee perceptions of distributive injustice and procedural injustice and also to lower employee reactions to whatever residual distributive and procedural injustice perceptions the employee may have. Exercise 2 and Exercise 3, which may facilitate a manager's assessment and enhancement of organizational justice in an actual workplace, follow.

Exercise 2: Assessing and enhancing organizational justice level in your organization

This exercise will facilitate the assessment of the present levels of distributive justice, procedural justice, and interactional justice in your organization. It will also draw your attention to the likely causes and consequences of the present levels of distributive justice, procedural justice, and interactional justice in your organization. This exercise will also facilitate your reflections on the possible actions for enhancing the levels of distributive justice, procedural justice, and interactional justice in your organization.

Consider the description of distributive justice, procedural justice, and interactional justice outlined in the earlier parts of this chapter. Based on these descriptions, make a thoughtful judgment of the level – high, moderate, low – at which distributive justice, procedural justice, and interactional justice is present in your organization. Based on these judgments of yours about the level of three forms of justice present in your organization, also make a judgment of the level at which overall organizational justice – consisting of distributive justice, procedural justice, and interactional justice – is present in your organization. Based on this assessment, respond to the following statements.

1. Indicate whether the overall level of organizational justice in your organization is high, moderate, or low.
2. Indicate whether the overall level of distributive justice in your organization is high, moderate, or low.
3. Indicate whether the overall level of procedural justice in your organization is high, moderate, or low.
4. Indicate whether the overall level of interactional justice in your organization is high, moderate, or low.
5. Describe what factors are responsible for the current level of distributive justice in your organization.
6. Describe what factors are responsible for the current level of procedural justice in your organization.
7. Describe what factors are responsible for the current level of interactional justice in your organization.
8. Describe how the current level of distributive justice, procedural justice, and interactional justice are likely to be affecting employees in your organization.
9. Describe how employees in your organization are likely to be reacting to the current justice levels in your organization.
10. Describe whether there is need to enhance in your organization:

    a. Distributive justice
    b. Procedural justice
    c. Interactional justice

11. Indicate what the desired level is of each of the following in your organization:

    a. Distributive justice: High or Low?
    b. Procedural justice: High or Low?
    c. Interactional justice: High or Low?

12. Describe how distributive justice level can be enhanced in your organization.
13. Describe how procedural justice level can be enhanced in your organization.
14. Describe how interactional justice level can be enhanced in your organization.

Exercise 3: Role play on dealing with an employee who experienced distributive injustice

Directions: This exercise has three parts, namely Part A, Part B, and Part C. For Part A, read the situation and prepare an action plan as directed at the end of Part A. Then for Part B, read the situation and prepare an action plan as directed at the end of Part B. Thereafter in Part C, complete the table as directed and answer the questions below the table.

Part A: The situation from a manager's perspective

You are in charge of the accounting department. One of your subordinates, Daniel, feels that he has experienced injustice. He is an accounting clerk. He received only 2% of his basic salary as an annual pay raise this year. Another accounting clerk, Kushal, who works with Daniel, received 4% of his basic salary as an annual pay raise. Daniel has begun to come late, be irritable, and complain at work since the annual pay increases were announced. You also noted that he clearly feels frustrated and angry. You were concerned about these reactions of Daniel because this could affect his performance, harmony in your work unit, and overall performance and climate in your work unit. Both Daniel and Kushal joined your organization a little over one year ago, and this is the first instance of their receiving an annual pay increase. You inquired with the HR department and learned that Kushal has acquired training in using a computerized accounting system and can work on both manual and computerized systems, whereas Daniel did not acquire this training and thus cannot use a computerized accounting system. Having been able to use both computerized and manual accounting systems, Kushal handled transactions of a much larger number of customer accounts than did Daniel. HR department's pay raise calculation formula was applied to both of them, and based on factors such as skill range demonstrated, quantity of output produced, and self-development that are considered in the formula, the pay increases given to both of them were just. Now you would like to have a discussion with Daniel so that his negative reactions do not continue and so that he is motivated to put in increased effort.

Your task for Part A

1. Prepare an action plan of how you would conduct the discussion session with Daniel. Your plan should include the manner in which you would conduct the discussion and the exact nature of information that you would provide to him. You may make brief written notes to carry with you to guide you through the discussion.
2. After writing your notes, read Part B "Experience the Situation from the Employee's Perspective."

Part B: Experience the situation from the employee's perspective

You are Daniel. You have been working as an accounting clerk for this organization for a little over one year now. You and Kushal work as accounting clerks at neighboring work stations in the office. Both of you have a B.Com degree, are qualified to do the accounting work, and joined the organization a little over one year ago. You work as hard as Kushal. The quality of work (e.g., number of errors) produced by both of you is nearly the same. Your regularity in attendance and your willingness to stay back after office hours to complete extra work have been somewhat better than Kushal's. Also, you have a little more experience in accounting work from the period prior to joining this organization and hence you help new clerks more than Kushal does. Last month, as a part of the organization's annual pay raise decision, you received 2% of your basic salary as your annual pay increase. A few days after that, while having lunch with Kushal, he mentioned that he had received 4% of his basic salary as his annual pay raise. You were shocked to hear this because you had expected your annual pay raise to be equal or a little higher than his. On the contrary, you learned that his annual pay raise was twice that of yours. After the lunch break, anger gradually increased in you; you felt hurt. You also became concerned about what will happen to you here in the future. You have your old parents and your own family to support. There are other financial commitments such as installments on your household appliances and bank loan repayment for the housing loan. Anger and worry preoccupied your mind in the following days. Your usual courtesy toward your coworkers is not being expressed and anger comes out in your interactions with them. You do not know what to do to rectify this unjust pay increase situation. You just feel like avoiding your place of work and have begun to come in a little late and when you speak to others your helplessness and anger come out in your complaints. A few minutes ago, your manager mentioned to you that he would like to have a discussion with you. You feel that this discussion would be about the pay raise instance.

Your task for Part B

1. Now, after experiencing the situation from the employee's perspective and thus having received some additional information, prepare an action plan on how you would conduct the discussion session with Daniel. Your plan should include the manner in which you will conduct the discussion and the exact nature of information that you would provide to him. You may make brief written notes to carry with you to guide you through the discussion.
2. After writing your notes, complete Part C.

Part C: assessing your adequacy in addressing justice aspects

Your task for Part C

Complete the tasks specified in items 1 to 4 below.

1. Read your action plan notes prepared in Part A and indicate in column A the level of adequacy (high, moderate, low) with which you had planned to address, in your action plan for Part A, each of the following justice aspects. Thereafter, read your action plan notes prepared in Part B and indicate in column B the level of adequacy (high, moderate, low) with which you had planned to address, in your action plan for Part B, each of the following justice aspects.

No.	Justice Aspect	Column A (Use for Part A)	Column B (Use for Part B)
I	**Distributive justice**		
a	Inputs		
b	Outcomes		

No.	Justice Aspect	Column A (Use for Part A)	Column B (Use for Part B)
c	Outcome-input ratio in comparison to other employee		
2	**Procedural justice**		
a	Accuracy of information used		
b	Consistency in the application of procedures		
c	Absence of bias in the use of procedures		
d	Presence of appeal process to correct errors in decisions		
e	Providing employees a say in the decision process		
3	**Interactional justice**		
a	Providing justifications		
b	Providing excuses		
c	Providing apologies		
d	Being truthful and honest		
e	Being courteous and respectful		
f	Listening to the employee		

Note: The contents of the above table are partly based on have come from various sources including Adams (1963, 1965), Colquitt (2001), Cropanzano et al. (2007, p. 36), Folger and Konovsky (1989, p. 117, 120, 121), Greenberg descriptions of justice forms in Greenberg [1987, 2009]; experimental treatment content description in Greenberg [1990, 1993]; and supervisory training contents in Greenberg [2006], and Masterson et al. (2000), Moorman (1991, p. 850). Aspects listed under procedural justice category are based on the features of procedures described in the literature as emerging from two works (Leventhal, 1980 and Leventhal, Karuza, and/or Fry, 1980, as cited and outlined in various works such Greenberg, 1987, p. 14–15; Greenberg, 2009, p. 256–257; Masterson et al., 2000, p. 730; Moorman, 1991, p. 847). Aspects listed under interactional justice category are based on the features of interactional justice described in the literature as emerging from two works (Bies, 1987 and/or Bies and Moag, 1986, as cited and outlined in various works such as Greenberg, 1987, p. 17; Greenberg, 2009, p. 257–258; Masterson et al., 2000, p. 739, 741; Moorman, 1991, p. 847). The aspects listed under various justice categories in the above table are also based on the description in the preceding parts of this chapter.

2. Compare your responses in Column A and B and assess whether the level of adequacy in your addressing justice aspects improved after doing Part B ("Experience the situation from the employee's perspective"). Based on this, reflect whether you

can more adequately understand and address justice aspects by interacting with the employees who have experienced injustice.
3. Based on your responses in Column A and B, assess which justice aspects you addressed with a high level of adequacy and which justice aspects you need to pay attention to for addressing them with reasonable adequacy.
4. Based on your work on this exercise, reflect whether (a) interactional justice is under your control as a manager, (b) providing interactional justice can make employees more receptive to accepting unfavorable outcomes, (c) through interactions with employees you can address various justice aspects and enhance employees' perceptions of distributive justice, procedural justice, and interactional justice.

References

Adams, J. S. 1963. Toward an understanding of inequity. *Journal of Abnormal and Social Psychology*, 67(5): 422–436.
Adams, J. S. 1965. Inequity in social exchange. In L. Berkowitz (Ed.), *Advances in Experimental Social Psychology* (Vol. 2, pp. 267–299). Academic Press: New York, NY.
Allen, N. J. and Meyer, J. P. 1990. The measurement and antecedents of affective, continuance, and normative commitment to the organization. *Journal of Occupational Psychology*, 63: 1–18.
Cassar, V. and Buttigieg, S. C. 1015. Psychological contract breach, organizational justice and emotional well-being. *Personnel Review*, 44: 217–235.
Cohen-Charash, Y. and Spector, P. E. 2001. The role of justice in organizations: A meta-analysis. *Organizational Behavior and Human Decision Processes*, 86(2): 278–321.
Colquitt, J. A. 2001. On the dimensionality of organizational justice: A construct validation of a measure. *Journal of Applied Psychology*, 86: 386–400.
Colquitt, J. A., Conlon, D. E., Wesson, M. J., Porter, O. L. H. and Ng, K. Y. 2001. Justice at the millennium: A meta-analytic review of 25 years of organizational justice research. *Journal of Applied Psychology*, 80(3): 425–445.
Colquitt, J. A., Scott, B. A., Rodell, J. B., Long, D. M., Zapata, C. P., Colon, D. E., and Wesson, M. J. 2013. Justice at the milllennium, a decade later: A meta-analytic test of social exchange and affect-based perspectives. *Journal of Applied Psychology*, 98: 199–236.
Cropanzano, R., Bowen, D. E. and Gilliland, S. W. 2007. The management of organizational justice. *Academy of Management Perspectives*, 21(4): 34–48.

Cropanzano, R., Byrne, Z. S., Bobocel, D. R., and Rupp, D. E. 2001. Moral virtues, fairness heuristics, social entities, and other denizens of justice. *Journal of Vocational Behavior*, 58: 164–209.

Daniels, K. 2000. Measures of five aspects of affective well-being at work. *Human Relations*, 53(2): 275–294.

Folger, R. and Konovsky, M. A. 1989. Effects of procedural and distributive justice on reactions to pay raise decisions. *Academy of Management Journal*, 32: 115–130.

Goodman, P. and Friedman, A. 1969. An examination of quantity and quality of performance under conditions of overpayment in piece rate. *Organizational Behavior and Human Performance*, 4: 365–374.

Greenberg, J. 1987. A taxonomy of organizational justice theories. *Academy of Management Review*, 12(1): 9–22.

Greenberg, J. 1990. Employee theft as a reaction to underpayment inequity: The hidden costs of pay cuts. *Journal of Applied Psychology*, 72: 55–61.

Greenberg, J. 1993. Stealing in the name of justice: Informational and interpersonal moderators of theft reactions to underpayment inequity. *Organizational Behavior and Human Decision Processes*, 54: 81–103.

Greenberg, J. 2006. Losing sleep over organizational injustice: Attenuating insomniac reactions to underpayment inequity with supervisory training in interactional justice. *Journal of Applied Psychology*, 91: 58–69.

Greenberg, J. 2009. Promote procedural and interactional justice to enhance individual and organizational outcomes. In E. A. Locke (Ed.), *Handbook of Principles of Organizational Behavior* (pp. 255–271). John Wiley & Sons: West Sussex.

Judge, T. A., Thoresen, C. J., Bono, J. E. and Patton, G. K. 2001. The job satisfaction-job performance relationship: A qualitative and quantitative review. *Psychological Bulletin*, 127: 376–407.

Keyes, C. L. M., Shmotkin, D. and Ryff, C. D. 2002. Optimizing well-being: The empirical encounter of two traditions. *Journal of Personality and Social Psychology*, 82: 1007–1022.

Konovsky, M. A. 2000. Understanding procedural justice and its impact on business organizations. *Journal of Management*, 26(3): 489–511.

Konovsky, M. A. and Pugh, S. D. 1994. Citizenship behavior and social exchange. *Academy of Management Journal*, 37: 656–669.

Lee, A. and Cropanzano, R. 2009. Do East Asians respond more/less strongly to organizational justice than North Americans: A meta-analysis. *Journal of Management Studies*, 46: 787–805.

Locke, E. A. 2003. Good definitions: The epistemological foundation of scientific progress. In J. Greenberg (Ed.), *Organizational Behavior: The State of the Science* (pp. 415–444). Lawrence Erlbaum Associates: Mahwah, NJ.

Masterson, S. S., Lewis, K., Goldman, B. M. and Taylor, M. S. 2000. Integrating justice and social exchange: The differing effects of fair procedures and treatment on work relationships. *Academy of Management Journal*, 43(4): 738–748.

McFarlin, D. B. and Sweeney, P. D. 1992. Distributive and procedural justice as predictors of satisfaction with personal and organizational outcomes. *Academy of Management Journal*, 35(3): 626–637.

Moorman, R. H. 1991. Relationship between organizational justice and organizational citizenship behaviors: Do fairness perceptions influence employee citizenship? *Journal of Applied Psychology*, 76: 845–855.

Moorman, R. H., and Byrne, Z. S. 2005. How Does Organizational Justice Affect Organizational Citizenship Behavior? In J. Greenberg and J. A. Colquitt (Eds.), *Handbook of Organizational Justice* (pp. 355–380). Lawrence Erlbaum: Mahwah, NY.

Moorman, R. H., Blakely, G. L. and Niehoff, B. P. 1998. Does perceived organizational support mediate the relationship between procedural justice and OCB. *Academy of Management Journal*, 41(3): 351–357.

Podsakoff, P. M., Mackenzie, S. B., Paine, J. B. and Bacharach, D. G. 2000. Organizational citizenship behaviors: A critical review of the theoretical and empirical literature and suggestions for future research. *Journal of Management*, 26(3): 513–563.

Rupp, D. E., Shao, R., Jones, K. S., Liao, H. 2014. The utility of a multifoci approach to the study of organizational justice: A meta-analytic investigation into the consideration of normative rules, moral accountability, bandwidth-fidelity, and social exchange. *Organizational Behavior and Human Decision Processes*, 123: 159–185.

Sashkin, M. and Williams, R. L. 1990. Does fairness make a difference? *Organizational Dynamics*, 19(2): 56–71.

Skitka, L. J., Winquist, J., and Hutchinson, S. 2003. Are outcome fairness and outcome favorability distinguishable psychological constructs? A meta-analytic review. *Social Justice Research*, 16: 309–341.

Viswesvaran, C. and Ones, D. S. 2202. Examining the construct of organizational justice: A meta-analytic evaluation of relations with work attitudes and behaviors. *Journal of Business Ethics*, 38: 193–203.

Whitman, D. S., Caleo, S., Carpenter, N. C., Horner, M. T. and Bernerth, J. B. 2012. Fairness at collective level: A meta-analytic examination of the consequences of boundary conditions of organizational justice climate. *Journal of Applied Psychology*, 97: 776–791.

Chapter 7

Organizational support for employee performance and well-being

Exercise 1: Developing a preliminary understanding of employee beliefs of organizational support

Assume that you are transferred by your organization to a very distant location in a different region of the country. Culture there is quite different from the culture of the place you have lived so far. You do not know the customs, norms, people, and resources to fulfill your life requirements (stores for buying necessities, schools, hospitals, etc.). You will come across some people in your workplace and in the society there. You need to decide with whom to form more close relationships and whom to avoid so that you can comfortably live there. How will you go about deciding this? Let us consider this below.

In the above situation, you have various needs. You need information about the local community and culture, about where and how to obtain necessities, about which stores are good, and about which hospitals are good and accessible. You will also need various kinds of help, such as someone to provide you a vehicle, offer a place to stay on a temporary basis, help you in an emergency situation, and provide you with social support. Many of these help requirements reflect your needs. These needs and associated help requirements may not emerge, but you need to anticipate their likelihood and have people around you who can help you when such needs arise. Thus, to identify such people who may help you when needed, you may consider information on who inquires about your comforts, shows concerns for your feelings, and expresses willingness to provide you what you need. After identifying such people, you are likely to start forming close relationships with those people who seem to be ready to fulfill your various needs in this new location where you have been newly transferred. This is what tends to happen in an individual's formation of social relationships with others. A similar process can occur in an employee's formation of a relationship with his/her organization. An employee is likely to assess whether the organization has a high or low level of readiness to fulfill his/her need for recognition, need for rewards, etc., and based on his/her assessment of the level of organizational readiness, he/she will form a close or distant relationship with the organization. This employee belief about an organization's readiness to fulfill his/her needs is the belief or perception of organizational support. The details of employee belief of organizational support are described below.

Employee beliefs of organizational support

Employees expect their needs to be fulfilled by the organization (Shore and Tetrick, 1991, p. 641). They come to work for an organization so that they can obtain money, job security, skill development, career growth, recognition, happy experiences, belongingness, etc. These outcomes employees seek from an organization can be broadly categorized as outcomes fulfilling economic needs (e.g., money), emotional needs (e.g., happy experiences), and social needs (e.g., belongingness). As employees are concerned about seeking their needs fulfillment from an organization, they form expectations about their organization's willingness to fulfill their economic, emotional, and social needs, and this expectation is referred to as employee beliefs or perceptions of organizational support (Eisenberger, Huntington, Hutchison, and Sowa, 1986). Thus, employee beliefs of organizational support convey to them that the organization is concerned about their happiness and appreciates their contributions (Eisenberger et al., 1986).

To identify some of the basic features of employee beliefs of organizational support, the following three aspects can be noted. First, an employee belief of organizational support reflects the employee's belief that the organization has commitment to him/her (e.g., Eisenberger, et al. 1986, p. 500, 501; Kottke and Sharafinski, 1988, p. 1075; Shore and Tetrick, 1991, p. 637; Shore and Wayne, 1993, p. 774). Second, an employees' commitment to an organization reflects the employee's emotional and non-instrumental attachment to the organization, to its goals and values and, and to his/her role associated with the organizational goals and values (Buchanan, 1974, p. 533). It also reflects an employee's urge to put in substantial effort for the organization and to remain with the organization (Steers, 1977, p. 46). Third, in light of these features of commitment and that employee beliefs of organizational support reflect employee beliefs of an organization's commitment to him/her, employee beliefs of organizational support suggest that the organization is emotionally attached to him/her for non-instrumental or noncalculative considerations, recognizes his goals and values, and has an urge to fulfill its role or obligation for facilitating those goals and values of his/her. This view of organizational support directly reflecting of viewing organizational support as an organization's commitment to an employee is adopted in putting together the scale in the end-of-chapter exercise.

Why employees form beliefs of organizational support

As described in the chapter-opening example situation, in an interpersonal relationship, a person forms a belief about whether another person is kind or supportive. If a person's belief is that another person is kind and supportive, he/she is likely to expect that in his/her various situations of need-fulfilment requirements, another person will make positive responses. For example, he/she will expect that if he/she has a health problem, the kind and supportive person will advise him/her about the medical help available; if he/she has financial difficulty, the kind and supportive person may lend some money to him/her; and if he/she is feeling sad, the supportive person may help him/her to cheer up. Such expectations of a person that another person will fulfill his/her economic (e.g., money-related) needs emotional, and social needs are based on his/her belief that another person is kind to and supportive of him/her.

A similar process of viewing organization as an entity similar to a person or the process of "personification (e.g., Wayne, Shore, and Liden, 1997, p. 87; Shore and Tetrick, 1991, p. 641) is likely to happen in an employee's relationship with an organization. When an employee develops the belief of organizational support, he/she will form various expectations of the organization's likely positive responses to his/her requirements and difficult situations. For example, he/she will expect that if he/she has a work problem, the organization will try to solve it; if he/she is ill, the organization may provide him/her a less strenuous job or provide him/her leave; and if he/she puts in extra effort, the organization will provide recognition for it. Such various expectations of employees about how the organization will respond to him/her in various future situations are likely to be formed based on employee beliefs of organizational support (e.g., Wayne et al., 1997, p. 83). Thus, being able to hold various expectations about the organization's likely responses toward one's need fulfillment requirements in various future situations is a likely reason why employees form beliefs of organizational support.

How employees form beliefs of organizational support

Consider the following situation. At home, family A is one of your neighbors. Once you provided a delicious food plate to family A and after some time, only the empty plate, without any food items from their family, was returned to you by the wife from family A. On another occasion, when a child in family A was ill, you gave the child's father some medicines for the child, but when your child was ill, the father in family A did not offer any help. From such variety of behaviors of various individual members of family A experienced by you over time in different situations, you will form a belief that family A does not appreciate what you provide to them and is not interested in your well-being. You will form a belief that family A is not supportive of you. Thus, your belief of family A's support is formed from how various members of family A treated you in different situations at different points in time. It may be noted that the treatment was provided to you by different members of family A and at different points in time, but the attributions of supportiveness were made to the entire family A as an entity. Thus, the acts performed by various members of family A and at different points in time were aggregated into an overall assessment of supportiveness or nonsupportiveness of the entire family A as a single entity.

In a similar manner, employees in an organization receive treatment from various officials of an organization in a variety of situations. For example, there can be a situation where an employee needs to transfer to a job that is more suitable for his/her skills, but the human resources manager refuses to transfer him/her. In another situation in which the employee was ill, his/her supervisor refused to assign less strenuous work, even when such assignment would have been feasible. In yet another situation, a top management member told him/her that it would recruit another person in his/her place, because he/she had taken a few days of leave on account of his recent illness. From such various treatment by various officials – in the above examples, a human resources manager, a supervisor, a top management member – of an organization over various situations, the employee is likely form the belief of low organizational kindness or supportiveness (e.g., Wayne et al. 1997, p. 87). Such employee belief of organizational kindness or supportiveness can then influence the employee's feelings, motivation, and actions toward the organization, just as your feelings, motivation, and actions toward your neighbor are likely to be affected by your belief about the extent to which the neighbor is supportive and kind toward you.

How employee belief of organizational support influences employee feelings, motivation, and actions

In general, human beings follow the norm of reciprocity (Gouldner, 1960). The norm of reciprocity suggests, "(1) people should help those who have helped them, and (2) people should not injure those who have helped them" (Gouldner, 1960, p. 171). One of the reasons for such orientation toward the benefit provider is that when a person receives benefits from others, he/she feels a sense of indebtedness, and this creates a felt obligation to benefit the benefit provider (Gouldner, 1960).

Just as the norm of reciprocity influences an individual's orientation toward the person providing benefits to him/her, the norm of reciprocity is also likely to influence an employee's orientation toward his/her organization depending on the extent to which an employee believes that the organization has supported or benefitted him/her e.g., (Shore and Tetrick, 1991, p. 641; Shore and Wayne, 1993, p. 775). When an employee forms the belief of organizational support, there is an underlying belief that the organization is committed to him/her has treated him/her supportively and benefitted him/her in various situations in the past (e.g., Shore et al., 1997, p. 83, 87). Under the influence of norm of reciprocity, "when one party benefits another, an obligation is generated. The recipient is now indebted to the donor, and he remains so until he repays (Gouldner, 1960, p. 174)." Thus, an employee's belief of having received benefits from an organization and the influence of the norm of reciprocity are jointly likely to create an obligation in an employee to benefit the organization (e.g., Setton, Bennett, and

Liden, 1996, p. 219). An employee's felt obligation to benefit an organization is likely to motivate the employee to perform positive actions to benefit the organization. Indeed, empirical evidence is supportive of the suggestion that employee beliefs of organizational support create a felt obligation in an employee to benefit the organization and result in employees' positive contributions to the organization in terms of employees' organizational citizenship behaviors (e.g. Eisenberger, Armeli, Rexwinkel, Lynch, and Rhoades, 2001; Wayne et al., 1997).

Further, as employee belief of organizational support implies that the organization values the employee's contribution, the employee is likely to believe that his/her extra effort will be rewarded by the organization (Eisenberger, Fasolo, and Davis-LaMastro, 1990). Consistent with this, empirical evidence supports the link between employee beliefs of organizational support and employees' calculative involvement or effort-reward expectancy (Eisenberger et al., 1990). Thus, an employee's belief about a strong link between their effort and organizational rewards is likely to enhance the employee's motivation to put in extra effort.

Finally, employee belief of organizational support reflects an employee's belief that the organization is committed to him/her (e.g., Shore and Wayne, 1993, p. 774). Such employee belief that the organization is committed to them or is supportive of them is likely to enhance employees' positive feelings and well-being. Consistent with this, empirical evidence supports a positive relationship between employee beliefs of organizational support and employees' positive mood (Eisenberger et al., 2001). Empirical evidence also indicates that organizational support can weaken the positive relationship between employees' exposure to certain stressful conditions and their negative mood (George, Reed, Ballard, Colin, Fielding, 1993).

Thus, employee beliefs of organizational support can enhance employees' positive feelings, organization-benefitting motivations, and organization-benefitting actions. Empirical evidence, some of which is outlined below, is consistent with this.

Empirical evidence on outcomes of employee beliefs of organizational support

Empirical research on the outcomes of organizational support indicates that employee beliefs of organizational support are linked to some outcomes related to employee performance and well-being (e.g., Masterson, Lewis, Goldman, and Taylor, 2000). The results of a review of about ten years of empirical research by Ahmed and Nawaz (2015, p. 871) found the positive association of the employee beliefs of organizational support with various outcomes including employee engagement, job satisfaction, and organizational citizenship behaviors. Employee beliefs of organizational support have a positive relationship with well-being-related outcomes of job satisfaction and positive mood at work and a negative relationship with strains (Rhoades and Eisenberger, 2002), and a negative relationship with work-life conflict, stress and burnout (Kurtesis, Eisenberger, Ford, Buffardi, Stewart, and Adis, 2017, p. 1872). Employee beliefs of organizational support are linked to employee performance as well. Empirical research has found that employee beliefs of organizational support are positively related to employees' in-role or task performance and positive extra-role or contextual performance (Kurtesis, et al., 2017, p. 1874; Rhoades and Eisenberger, 2002; Riggle, Edmondson, and Hansen, 2009, p. 1028). Further, employee beliefs of organizational support have a negative association with employees' intentions to quit (e.g., Ahmed and Nawaz, 2015, p. 871–872; Kurtessis et al., 2015, p. 1074; Rhoades and Eisenberger, 2002, p. 709; Riggle et al., 2009, p. 1028), and actual quitting, absenteeism, and employees' counterproductive behaviors at work or negative behaviors (e.g., Kurtessis et al., 2017, p. 1873–74). The review works cited here have reviewed empirical research covering a period of 10 years (Ahmed and Nawaz, 2015), 15 years (Rhoades and Eisenberger, 2002), 20 years (Riggle et al., 2009), and 26 years (Kuressis et al., 2017). The above outlined results from various reviews of empirical research collectively suggest that employee beliefs of organizational support are positively related to employees' task performance, organizational citizenship behaviors or contextual performance, and also to outcomes reflecting employee well-being; and are negatively related to employees' quitting intentions, quitting, absenteeism, and negative work behaviors.

Empirical evidence on factors influencing beliefs of organizational support

As the employee beliefs of organizational support emerge as a part of social exchange process (e.g., Wayne et al., 1997, p. 82), in general, any factor that conveys to employees that the organization is ready to fulfill their economic, emotional, and social needs can potentially enhance employee beliefs of organizational support. Thus, providing benefits to employees and showing concern for employees can enhance employee beliefs of organizational support. Thus, for example, Wayne et al (1997) found developmental experiences and promotions of employees and Shore et al. (2002) found recognition, inclusion, distributive justice, and procedural justice as having positive relations with employee perceptions of organizational support. Empirical research has found that organizational justice, favorable pay and job conditions, and supervisory support have a positive relationship, whereas perceived organizational politics has a negative relationship with employee beliefs of organizational support (Kurtesis, et al., 2017, p. 1860, 1862; Rhoades and Eisenberger, 2002). The results of review of about ten years of empirical research by Ahmed and Nawaz (2015, p. 871) found a positive association of employee beliefs of organizational support and the organizational aspects of procedural justice, distributive justice, decision making participation, perception of autonomy, opportunities for growth, variety in tasks done, job security, support from coworkers, and supervisory support. Further, a more recent and comprehensive review of empirical research (Kurtessis et al., 2017 p. 1864–1866), which reviewed research studies done in a period of 26 years, found that enriching job characteristics as a category (which may include scope for applying a variety of skills on a job, availability of job performance-related feedback and scope for doing a whole and identifiable set of tasks), developmental opportunities in an organization, participation in decision making, and perceptions that organizational practices are family supportive also enhance employee beliefs of organizational support.

Some other factors influencing the emergence and consequences of beliefs of organizational support

Empirical research has found that when employees receive favorable job conditions, employee beliefs of organizational support are enhanced to a greater extent when employees feel that the organization has discretionarily provided the favorable job conditions (Eisenberger, Cummings, Armeli, and Lynch, 1997). Further, employee belief of organizational support is more strongly related to employees' felt obligation to benefit the organization when employees have high socio-emotional needs (Armeli, Eisenberger, Fasolo, and Lynch, 1998) and high adherence to the belief in maintaining with an organization an exchange of effort and rewards – reciprocation ideology (Eisenberger et al., 2001).

Further, literature suggests that when an individual receives benefits, his/her felt obligation to benefit the benefit provider depends on factors that include a benefit provider's provision of benefits "without thought of gain" (Gouldner, 1960, p. 171). This suggests that when employees see organizational benefits provision as free from the intents to manipulate, employees are likely to experience a high level of felt obligation to benefit the organization.

The preceding discussion of the factors influencing employee beliefs of organizational support can provide inputs on the possible actions managers can take to enhance employee beliefs of organizational support. The end-of-the chapter exercise provided below will facilitate reflection on some actions for enhancing employee beliefs of organizational support.

Exercise 2

Exercise 2: Self-assessment of employee beliefs of organizational support (Part A)

Directions: Listed below are a set of statements describing your beliefs about how an organization may deal with its employees. For each statement, indicate the extent to which you agree that the statement describes how your organization deals with you. Indicate 1 if you 'strongly disagree,' 2 if you 'disagree,' 3 if you 'neither agree nor disagree,' 4 if you 'agree,' and 5 if you 'strongly agree.' The numbers 1 to 5 in the right column response format have the meanings as outlined in the following response format.

1	2	3	4	5
Strongly Disagree	Disagree	Neither Agree nor Disagree	Agree	Strongly Agree

Statement	Response Format				
	1	2	3	4	5
1 Most of the organizational authorities are supportive of me.					
2 In most of my difficult situations the organization has been supportive of me.					

Statement	Response Format				
	1	2	3	4	5
3 The organization is committed to me as its member.					
4 The organization tries to make my membership of it a positive experience for me.					
5 The organization makes my membership of it beneficial for me.					
6 The organization views me as its member and not just as an employee.					

Note: The above items are partly based on the view that an employee's belief of organizational support is an employee's belief that the organization has commitment to him/her (e.g., Eisenberger et al., 1986, p. 500-501; Kottke and Sharafinski, 1988, p. 1075; Shore and Tetrick, 1991, p. 637; Shore and Wayne, 1993, p. 774). The above items are also based on the description in the preceding parts of this chapter. This is a rudimentary set of items prepared only for the purpose of this exercise.

Exercise 2: Scoring based on self-assessment (Part B)

Scoring guidelines to arrive at scores from Part A

After you complete marking responses to the statements in the scale in Part A, add the scores of all 6 items.

Write here the total of the scores of statements 1 to 6:_____
(Guideline: 6–10 = low; 11–20 = moderate; 21–30 = high)

Exercise 2: Beliefs of organizational support – Questions for reflection (Part C)

Note: In light of your scores on individual statements in Part A, total score in Part B, and actual conditions in your organization, answer the following questions. The initial questions focus on your own level of organizational support, while the subsequent questions focus on the organizational support experienced by most of the employees in your organization.

Kindly respond to the following statements to facilitate your reflection based on self-assessment.

1   Indicate your overall level of organizational support (low/ moderate/high).

2 Describe how you feel about your organizational support level.
3 Describe how the level of your organizational support affects your feelings about your work in your organization.
4 Describe how the level of your organizational support affects your work in your organization.
5 Indicate the likely level of organizational support for most of the employees in your organization (low/moderate/high).
6 Indicate the level of organizational support you would like for most of the employees in your organization (low/moderate/high).
7 Describe what actions you can take to enhance the level of organizational support for most of the employees in your organization.

References

Ahmed, I, and Nawaz, M. M. 2015. Antecedents and outcomes of perceived organizational support: A literature review approach. *Journal of Management Development*, 34: 867–880.

Armeli, S., Eisenberger, R., Fasolo, P. and Lynch, P. 1998. Perceived organizational support and police performance: The moderating influence of socioemotional needs. *Journal of Applied Psychology*, 83(2): 288–297.

Buchanan, B. 1974. Building organizational commitment: The socialization of managers in work organization. *Administrative Science Quarterly*, 19: 533–546.

Eisenberger, R., Armeli, S., Rexwinkel, B., Lynch, P. D. and Rhoades, L. 2001. Reciprocation of perceived organizational support. *Journal of Applied Psychology*, 80: 42–51.

Eisenberger, R., Cummings, J., Armeli, S. and Lynch, P. 1997. Perceived organizational support, discretionary treatment, and job satisfaction. *Journal of Applied Psychology*, 82: 812–820.

Eisenberger, R., Fasolo, P. and Davis-LaMastro, V. 1990. Perceived organizational support and employee diligence, commitment, and innovation. *Journal of Applied Psychology*, 75: 51–59.

Eisenberger, R., Huntington, R., Hutchison, S. and Sowa, D. 1986. Perceived organizational support. *Journal of Applied Psychology*, 71: 500–507.

George, J.M., Reed, T. F., Ballard, K. A., Colin, J., and Fielding, J. 1993. Contact with AIDS patents as a source of work-related distress: Effects of organizational and social support. *Academy of Management Journal*, 36: 157–171.

Gouldner, A. W. 1960. The norm of reciprocity: A preliminary statement. *American Sociological Review*, 25: 161–178.

Kottke, J. L. and Sharafinski, C. E. 1988. Measuring perceived supervisory and organizational support. *Educational and Psychological Measurement*, 48: 1075–1079.

Kurtesis, J. N., Eisenberger, R., Ford, M. T., Buffardi, L. C., Stewart, K. A., and Adis, C. S. 2017. Perceived organizational support: A meta-analytic evaluation of organizational support theory. *Journal of Management*, 43: 1854–1984.

Masterson, S. S.; Lewis, K; Goldman, B. M., & Taylor, M. S. 2000. Integrating justice and social exchange: The differing effects of fair procedures and treatment on work relationships. *Academy of Management Journal*, 43(4): 738–748.

Rhoades, L. and Eisenberger, R. 2002. Perceived organizational support: A review of the literature. *Journal of Applied Psychology*, 87(4): 698–714.

Riggle, R. J, Edmondson, D. R. and, Hansen, J. D. 2009. A meta-analysis of the relationship between perceived organizational support and job outcomes: 20 years of research. *Journal of Business Research*, 62: 1027–1030.

Settoon, R. P., Nathan, B., and Liden, R. C. 1996. Social exchange in organizations: Perceived organizational support, leader-member exchange, and employee reciprocity. *Journal of Applied Psychology*, 81: 219–227.

Shore, L. M. and Tetrick, L. E. 1991. A construct validity study of the Survey of Perceived Organizational Support. *Journal of Applied Psychology*, 76: 637–643.

Shore, L. M. and Wayne, S. J. 1993. Commitment and employee behavior: Comparison of affective commitment and continuance commitment with perceived organizational support. *Journal of Applied Psychology*, 78: 774–780.

Steers, R. M. 1977. Antecedents and outcomes of organizational commitment. *Administrative Science Quarterly*, 22: 46–56.

Wayne, S. J., Shore, L. M., and Liden, R. C. 1997. Perceived organizational support and leader-member exchange: A social exchange perspective. *Academy of Management Journal*, 40: 82–111.

Wayne, S. J., Shore, L. M., Bommer, W. H., and Tetrick, L. E. 2002. The role of fair treatment and rewards in perceptions of organizational support and leader-member exchange. *Journal of Applied Psychology*, 87: 590–598.

Chapter 8

Workplace spirituality for employee performance and well-being

Spiritual need as a human need

Human beings have several needs. Human beings require air, food, water, and sleep. The requirement of human beings for these resources is referred to as the physical needs of human beings. Thus, human beings have physical needs or a need for resources that maintain their physical being. Human beings also have an urge or need to go beyond the physical or material aspects in their functioning. The need of human beings to go beyond the physical aspects is referred to as the "need for transcendence" (Ellison, 1983, p. 330). The term transcendent refers to the non-physical dimension (Ellison, 1983) of human existence. Thus, the need for transcendence is the need to go beyond the physical aspects of human existence. This need is distinct from other human needs. This is reflected in Ellison (1983, pp. 330–331, emphasis original), who notes,

> Campbell (1981), for example, suggests that well-being depends on the satisfaction of three basic kinds of need: The need for having, the need for relating, and the need for being. ... While Campbell's research and multiple need conception are helpful, he and his colleagues have ignored a fourth set of needs which might be termed as the *need for transcendence* [emphasis original]. This refers to the sense of well-being we experience when we find purposes to commit ourselves to which involve ultimate meaning for life. It refers to a *non-physical dimension of awareness and experience* [emphasis added] which can be best termed spiritual.

Consistent with this, Moberg and Brusek (1978, p. 313) note that a UN expert committee concluded that life expectancy depends as much on spiritual and moral values as on aspects such as food, medical services, and shelter. As the food, shelter, and medical services aspects focus on the physical or material aspects, the above observation of the UN expert committee reflects that the spiritual dimension is distinct from the physical or material dimension of human beings. Further, Moberg and Brusek (1978, p. 314) note a scholar's view which yields an interpretation that the spiritual dimension is a "non-material" dimension. A more explicit statement on spirituality as the pursuit of the need for transcendence comes from Paloutzian, Emmons, and Keortge (2003, p. 124), who state, "This need for transcendence expresses itself as what is commonly called 'spirituality.'" That spirituality is a basic feature of human beings is reflected in Paloutzian et al. (2003, p. 124), who note, "a built-in tendency toward spirituality that is part of what makes a person human." This suggests that spirituality is seeking the fulfillment of the spiritual needs or needs for transcendence. This also suggests that spirituality is a feature of human beings.

Another perspective on spirituality as a part of human beings comes from Chandler, Holden, and Kolander (1992). Chandler et al. (1992, p. 168) note, 'Several psychological models include spirituality in their concepts of the nature of persons. Maslow (1971) contended that "the spiritual life (the contemplative, 'religious,' philosophical, or value-life) is ... part of human essence ... a defining characteristic of human nature' (p. 325). In his study of optimally functioning people, he labeled those at the top of his hierarchy 'transcendent self-actualizers.' Chandler et al. (1992, p. 169) further note that "Maslow (1971) ... thought motivation to achieve the metaneeds (self-actualization and self-transcendence) to be 'less urgent or demanding, weaker (than) basic needs' (Maslow, 1980, p. 125)."

Thus, the various views outlined above indicate that human beings have a spiritual need. They also indicate that the spiritual need refers to the need for transcendence or for going beyond the physical or material dimension of life.

Spiritual need or need for transcendence: need for going beyond oneself

The word "transcendent" refers to "stepping back from and moving beyond what is" (Ellison, 1983, p. 331). The term transcendent "means literally to 'climb over' or, more colloquially, to achieve a 'peak experience' or find one's 'higher self' (c.f. Maslow 1954, 1968)" (Mirvis, 1997, p. 197). From these expressions, various interpretations of the need for transcendence or need for spirituality or spiritual need come out.

First, the term transcendent has meanings such as going beyond or stepping up from. These meanings raise a question: Going beyond or climbing up from what? As the "transcendence" needs refer to the non-physical aspect (e.g., Ellison, 1983) or nonmaterial aspect (e.g., Moberg and Brusek, 1978) of human existence, to transcend is to go beyond or step up from one's physical self or material self. As it is ordinarily inconceivable for a human being to disengage from one's physical self or material self, to transcend here seems to imply to go beyond one's physical or material interests or to go beyond one's self-interests. This is consistent with Ellison's (1983, p. 338) view of transcendence as the "capacity to find purpose and meaning beyond one's self and the immediate." Thus, the transcendence needs or spiritual needs refer to going beyond one's self and one's material self-interests.

The plausibility of the view of spiritual needs as going beyond one's material self-interests can be seen in various descriptions or uses of the term spirituality. For example, consider the various meanings of spirituality provided in de Klerk (2005, pp. 65–66) as

> transcendence, balance, sacredness, altruism, meaning in life, living with a deep connectedness to the universe, and the awareness of something or some greater than oneself (God, or an energy force) that provides energy and wisdom that transcends the material aspects of life.

Also consider the various forms of "transcendent" values or needs mentioned in Kolodinsky, Giacalone, and Jurkiewicz (2008, p. 465) as the "need for connectedness, meaning, purpose, altruism, virtue, nurturance, and hope in one's work and at one's workplace." Aspects such as altruism, nurturance, and wisdom beyond the material facets of life included in these meanings or interpretations of the term spirituality or transcendence imply going beyond one's self or going beyond one's self-interests.

Second, one description of spiritual well-being is in terms of living life in harmony with self, community, environment, and God (Ellison, 1983, p. 331). This also implies going beyond self to function by relating oneself to others. Similarly, Chandler et al.

(1992, p. 169) define "spiritual" as "pertaining to the innate capacity to, and the tendency to seek to, transcend one's locus of centricity."

Third, functioning in the pursuit of the transcendent or what is "beyond" is termed as spirituality (Paloutzian et al., 2003, p. 124). This also suggests that seeking the transcendent, which is non-material, is spirituality. This suggests that spirituality involves going beyond material concerns or beyond material self-interests.

Thus, many views of spirituality suggest that it involves going beyond one's material concerns or material self-interests or self-interests. This raises a relevant question as to what going beyond self-interests implies or how one goes beyond one's self-interests. This aspect is considered below.

Spiritual need or need for transcendence: need for connecting with others and contributing to others

The above description indicates that spiritual need fulfillment involves going beyond one's material self-interests. One of the ways of going beyond one's material self-interests is connecting with and contributing to others. This is reflected in one view of spiritual development, which suggests that it is "the process of growing the intrinsic human capacity for self-transcendence, in which the self is embedded in something greater than the self, including the sacred. It is the developmental 'engine' that propels the search for connect-edness, meaning, purpose, and contribution" (Benson, Roehlkepar-tain, and Rude, 2003, pp. 205–206). Similarly, Greenberg (2002, p. 144) notes that spirituality involves experiences of transcenden-tal aspects of life and that the transcendent aspects include meaning and connectedness.

The above discussion suggests that spirituality involves tran-scendence or going beyond material self-interests. It also suggests that going beyond self-interests can be attained through aspects such as being connected with others and contributing to others (finding meaning). While the above discussion describes spirituality as a human experience in an overall life context, workplace spir-ituality refers to employee experiences of spirituality through work and in their workplace. Various aspects of employee experiences of workplace spirituality are described below.

Workplace spirituality

Workplace spirituality refers to employee experiences in the workplace that reflect the fulfillment of their spiritual needs. In the literature, meaning in work, community at work, compassion, transcendence, and mindfulness (e.g., Ashmos and Duchon, 2000; Petchsawanga and Duchon, 2009) are identified as some of the aspects of workplace spirituality experiences of employees. Kinjersky and Skrypnek (2006, p. 7) have identified engaging work, sense of community, mystical transcendence, and spiritual connection as the aspects of workplace spirituality.

Meaning in work or meaningful work refers to work that is meaningful from a cognitive perspective, joy-providing, and connected to the benefits of others and reflecting what is important in one's life (Duchon and Plowman, 2005, p. 814). Somewhat similar experiences are reflected in some of the items in the engaging work dimension identified by Kinjerski and Skrypnek (2006, p. 7). Community at work refers to the experience that one's relationships at work provide feelings of having mutual obligations, sharing with others, and having commitment to each other (Duchon and Plowman, 2005, p. 814). Somewhat similar experiences are reflected in the items in the sense of community dimension identified by Kinjerski and Skrypnek (2006, p. 7). Compassion refers to experiencing empathy for others and being sympathetic and helpful to alleviate the suffering of others at the workplace (Petchsawanga and Duchon, 2009). The items in the transcendence dimension of workplace spirituality (Petchsawanga and Duchon, 2009, p. 463) suggest that this dimension focuses on employee experiences such as joy, ecstasy, and vitality at work which are somewhat similar to the experiences reflected in the items in the mystical experience dimension identified by Kinjerski and Skrypnek (2006, p. 7). Mindfulness as a dimension of workplace spirituality reflects workplace experience of being aware of one's thoughts and actions at a particular moment and being focused in the present (Petchsawanga and Duchon, 2009). While these several forms of experiences are reflected in workplace spirituality, meaning in work and community at work are the main workplace spirituality dimensions considered in the literature (e.g., Albuquerque, Cunha, Martins, and Britosa, 2014; Saks, 2011).

As outlined above, the existing literature has identified various dimensions of workplace spirituality. However, it may be appropriate to identify workplace spirituality dimensions by considering some of the key features of human spirituality outlined earlier in this chapter. The first and second section in this chapter outlined, based on literature, that spiritual need is a basic human need and spiritual need is the need for self-transcendence. The third section in this chapter explained that spiritual need fulfillment or self-transcendence of human beings can be facilitated through connecting to others and contributing to others. Extending this nature of human spirituality in general to the specific phenomenon of workplace spiritualty – employees' spirituality experiences in workplace – suggests that workplace spirituality can be viewed as employees' experience of self-transcendence in the workplace by serving others/society through work and by serving coworkers through relationships in the workplace. This suggests that employees can experience self-transcendence in workplace through society-benefitting work and through coworker-benefitting relationships in the workplace. In light of this view coming from the description of individual spirituality in general and context-specific employee workplace spirituality experiences in the workplace, it is suggested here that employee workplace spirituality can be viewed as consisting of the two dimensions of: a) employees' self-transcendence through society-benefitting work and b) employees' self-transcendence through coworker-benefitting relationships in workplace. These dimensions are linked to a literature-based view of human spirituality and they also bear some similarity with the contents of and/or items in some of the workplace spirituality dimensions in the existing literature such as meaning at work and conditions for community (e.g., Ashmos and Duchon, 2000, p. 143; Duchon and Plowman, 2005, p. 812–814), sense of community (Milliman, Czaplewski, and Ferguson, 2003, p. 437), engaging work and sense of community (Kinjerski and Skrypnek, 2006, p. 7), meaningful work and compassion (Petchsawang and Duchon, 2009, p. 462). However, the two dimensions identified here, because of their explicit and nearly exclusive focus on the aspect of self-transcendence through an other-benefitting orientation in both work and in relationships at workplace, are somewhat different from those in the existing literature. In light of the above, these two dimensions – employees' self-transcendence through society-benefitting work and through coworker-benefitting relationships in workplace – are used in the exercise at the end of the chapter which can facilitate assessment of and reflection on enhancing workplace spirituality in an organization.

Organizational outcomes of workplace spirituality

Managers are responsible for enhancing the performance and well-being of employees in their work units and organizations. Therefore, the utility of workplace spirituality for a manager needs to be assessed partly based on whether implementing workplace spirituality and providing workplace spirituality experiences to employees can improve employee performance and well-being. Some evidence generated over about the last decade and a half suggests that employee workplace spirituality experiences have a positive relationship with employee performance and well-being. Some of such empirical evidence is outlined below.

Workplace spirituality and employees' work attitudes

Workplace spirituality experiences fulfill employees' spiritual needs. Thus, workplace spirituality, by fulfilling employees' spiritual needs, can potentially enhance employees' positive feelings about the work and positive involvement in the work and the organization. Consistent with this, empirical research studies have found a positive relationship between employee experiences of workplace spirituality and employees' job satisfaction (e.g., Milliman et al., 2003; Pawar, 2009a). Research (e.g., Pawar, 2009a) also found a positive relationship between employee experiences of workplace spirituality and employees' job involvement. Employee workplace spirituality experiences are also positively associated with employees' affective commitment to an organization (e.g., Milliman et al., 2003; Pawar, 2009a).

Workplace spirituality and employees' well-being

Employee workplace spirituality experiences of meaning and community have been found to be positively associated with employees' mental well-being, healthy behavior, and spiritual well-being (McKee, Driscoll, Kelloway, and Kelley, 2011, p. 242). Further, the community in work has been found to be negatively associated with physiological ill-health symptoms (McKee et al., 2011, p. 242). Employee experiences of workplace spirituality have been found to have a positive association with employees' emotional well-being, psychological well-being, social well-being, and spiritual well-being (Pawar, 2016). This relationship between employee workplace spirituality experiences and multiple forms of employee well-being is important, as Grant, Christianson and Price (2007) note that organizational actions aimed at enhancing employee well-being enhance some form of employee well-being while simultaneously lowering some other forms of employee well-being. Thus, in contrast to such actions, enhancing employees' workplace spirituality experiences is a distinctly important action for managers, as it can simultaneously improve multiple forms of employee well-being without lowering any form of employee well-being.

Workplace spirituality and employee performance

Employee experiences of workplace spirituality are likely to have a positive influence on employee performance in two distinct ways. First, employee experiences of workplace spirituality are likely to influence employee performance through their positive influence on employees' job satisfaction and affective commitment. Second, employee experiences of workplace spirituality are likely to directly influence the performance. These two ways are outlined below.

First, research (e.g., Milliman et al., 2003; Pawar, 2009a) has, as outlined above, revealed that workplace spirituality has positive association with employees' affective commitment and job satisfaction. Employees' affective commitment is positively associated with employees' task performance (Allen and Meyer, 1996) and contextual performance or organizational citizenship behaviors (e.g., Allen and Meyer, 1996; Podsakoff, MacKenzie, Paine, and Bacharach, 2000). Employees' job satisfaction is positively associated with employees' task performance (Hoffman, Blair, Meriac, and Woehr, 2007; Petty, McGee, and Cavender, 1984) and contextual performance or organizational citizenship behaviors (e.g. Bateman and Organ, 1983; Hoffman et al., 2007). Thus, employee experiences of workplace spirituality, because of their positive association with employees' job satisfaction and affective commitment, are likely to have a positive effect on employees' task performance and contextual performance.

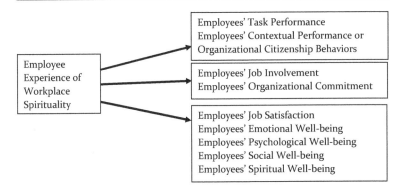

Figure 8.1 Some of workplace spirituality's performance and well-being outcomes

Source: Partly based on various works including Benefiel et al. (2014), Pawar (2009a), and Pawar (2016)

Second, a review of empirical research on workplace spirituality by Benefiel, Fry, and Geigle (2014) indicates that workplace spirituality has a positive association with employees' task performance and organizational citizenship behaviors, which is another term for contextual performance. This relationship is likely to be there for various reasons, such as employee workplace spirituality experience of meaning in work is likely to induce extra effort exertion by employees. This relationship is also likely to be there because employee workplace spirituality experiences, such as community at work, are likely to provide support to employees, which can enhance employees' performance.

The above-described various likely workplace spirituality outcomes of employee performance and well-being are depicted in Figure 8.1.

What factors enhance employee experiences of workplace spirituality?

From the review of workplace spirituality research (e.g., Geigle, 2012), it can be inferred that only a modest amount of empirical research exists on the factors enhancing employee experiences of workplace spirituality. However, the modest empirical research, some literature (e.g., Pawar, 2009b) outlining suggestions for enhancing employee workplace spirituality experiences exists.

Pawar (2009b), drawing upon the existing literature, outlined a conceptual model on the possible ways of enhancing employee experiences of workplace spirituality. This model from Pawar (2009b), reproduced in Figure 8.2, includes various ways such as enhancing individual spirituality of employees, making group-level interventions to enhance employee spirituality, facilitating spiritual development of leaders, enhancing spiritual values and practices of leaders, adopting spiritual values such as benevolence and justice in an organization, and adopting organizational practices which can enhance employees' individual spirituality, which can enhance workplace spirituality experiences.

Pawar (2008, p. 553), by comparing two existing examples in the literature (Chakraborty, 1993; Milliman, Ferguson, Trickett, and Condemi, 1999) on enhancing employee experiences of spirituality in organizations, suggested that two approaches can be characterized as "inside-out" or "individual-focused approach" and

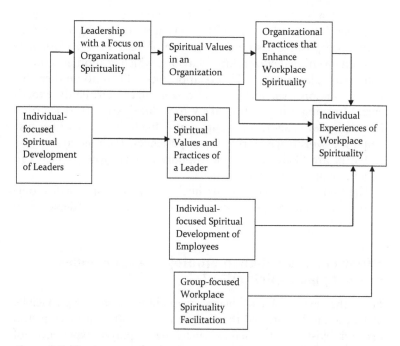

Figure 8.2: Some ways of enhancing employee experiences of workplace spirituality

Source: Reproduced with permission from Pawar (2009b), p. 382

"outside-in" or "organization-focused approach." The inside-out approach focuses on facilitating the development of individual spirituality or the inner side of employees and the enhanced individual spirituality of employees then can manifest in employee behaviors and organizational culture reflecting spiritual values Pawar (2008). The outside-in approach focuses on developing organizational features such as adopting a noble organizational cause that serves others or has positive organizational values and these features can then influence other aspects of organizational functioning and enhance employee experiences of workplace spirituality Pawar (2008). Thus, from the description in Pawar (2008) developing the spirituality level of individual employees and developing organizational features such as adopting spiritual values in an organization come out as two possible actions for enhancing employee workplace spirituality experiences. The details of the actual examples of the individual-focused and organization-focused approaches to workplace spirituality enhancement can be seen in Chakraborty (1993) and Milliman et al. (1999) respectively, and some of the similarities and differences between these two approaches are described in Pawar (2008).

Empirical evidence suggests that organizational spirituality has a stronger association than does employees' individual spirituality with employee experiences of workplace spirituality (Pawar, 2017). As the organization-focused approach can enhance organizational spirituality while the individual-focused approach can enhance individual spirituality Pawar (2008), the empirical evidence in Pawar (2017) suggests that the organization-focused approach is likely to be more efficacious than the individual-focused approach in enhancing employee experiences of workplace spirituality. However, this inference is merely suggestive, as this is only one study providing empirical evidence on this aspect.

Empirical evidence in Pawar (2014) indicates a positive relationship between individual spirituality of a leader and his/her leadership spiritual behaviors toward subordinates. This evidence provides some support for the likely link between individual spiritual development of a leader and a leader's spiritual practices shown in Figure 8.1.

The above description suggests various possible ways in which managers can enhance employee experiences of workplace spirituality. Further, within each way, there could be many possible actions. For example, one way of enhancing employee experiences of workplace spirituality is developing the individual spirituality of employees. As individual spiritual development could be facilitated by many actions, such as creative visualization, rhythmic breathing, and meditation (e.g., Chandler et al., 1992, p. 172–173), several actions can be considered by managers for implementing this way of enhancing employee experiences of workplace spirituality. Consistent with this possibility, a positive relationship has been observed between the frequency of employees' meditation practice and their experience of workplace spirituality (Petchsawanga and Duchon, 2012).

Enhancing employee experiences of workplace spirituality

From the description in the preceding parts of this chapter, managers are likely to develop an awareness of the requirement to provide workplace spirituality experiences to their employees for at least three reasons. First, the preceding description is likely to help managers realize that employees, as human beings, are likely to seek fulfillment of their spiritual needs in the workplace, and thus it is relevant for managers to provide employees workplace spirituality experiences. Thus, from a humanistic perspective, managers are likely to the see the requirement of providing to employees workplace spirituality experiences so that employees' spiritual needs get fulfilled in the workplace.

Second, the preceding description is likely to lead to managers' realization that providing workplace spirituality experiences to employees is likely to improve employees' job satisfaction, affective commitment to the organization, and job involvement. It is also likely to enhance employee well-being. Thus, from an employee welfare perspective, managers are likely to see the requirement of providing to employees workplace spirituality experiences.

Third, the preceding description is likely to point out to the managers that providing workplace spirituality experiences to employees is likely to enhance employees' task performance and contextual performance or organizational citizenship behaviors, which can benefit the organization. Thus, from a utilitarian perspective, managers are likely to see the requirement of providing to employees workplace spirituality experiences.

In light of the likely requirement of managers to provide workplace spirituality experiences to their employees, managers can take certain steps. First, managers can assess the current level of work-place spirituality in their organization or work unit. The scale in the end-of-chapter exercise can provide some guidance on doing this. Second, based on the current level of workplace spirituality in their organization, managers can consider various actions for enhancing workplace spirituality. Various ways of enhancing employee experiences of workplace spirituality shown in Figure 8.1 and the associated description can be used for exploring the possible actions. The end-of-chapter exercise will be useful for facilitating reflection on carrying out these steps.

Exercise 1

Exercise 1: Self-assessment of workplace spirituality (Part A)

Directions: Listed below are a set of statements about how you feel in your workplace or organization. For each statement, indicate to what extent you agree that the statement describes how you feel in your workplace or organization by circling only one response option. Circle 1 if you 'strongly disagree,' 2 if you 'disagree,' 3 if you 'neither agree nor disagree,' 4 if you 'agree,' and 5 if you 'strongly agree.' The numbers 1 to 5 in the right column labeled "Response Format" have the meanings as outlined in the following response format.

1	2	3	4	5
Strongly Disagree	Disagree	Neither Agree nor Disagree	Agree	Strongly Agree

Statement	Response Format				
	1	*2*	*3*	*4*	*5*
1 My work in the organization benefits many people.					
2 Through my work in the organization, I am serving society.					
3 My work in the organization contributes to the betterment of society.					

Statement	Response Format				
	1	2	3	4	5
4 In doing my work in the organization, I benefit the society.					
5 My work in the organization makes me think beyond my own benefits and gains.					
6 I feel I do something socially useful through the work that I perform in my organization.					
7 Through my relationships in this organization, I contribute a lot to my coworkers.					
8 Through my relationships in this organization, I benefit my coworkers.					
9 Through my relationships in this organization, I do good to my coworkers.					
10 In my relationships in this organization, I try to help my coworkers without seeking any material benefits for myself.					
11 Through my relationships in this organization, I serve my coworkers.					
12 Through my relationships in this organization, I try to promote welfare of my coworkers.					

Note: The above items are partly based on various works including Ashmos and Duchon (2000), Fry, Vitucci, and Cedillo (2005), Giacalone and Jurkiewicz (2003), Kinjerski and Skrypnek (2006) Milliman et al. (2003), Pawar (2009a) and Petchsawanga and Duchon (2009), and the items are particularly based on the description in the preceding parts of this chapter including the discussion which suggested employees' "self-transcendence through society-benefitting work" and "self-transcendence through coworker-benefitting relationships in workplace" as two dimensions of workplace spirituality with their explicit and nearly exclusive focus on self-transcendence through an other-benefitting orientation in both work and in relationships at workplace. This is a rudimentary set of items prepared only for the purpose of this exercise.

Exercise 1: Self-assessment of workplace spirituality (Part B)

Scoring Guidelines for the Instrument: After you complete marking responses to the statements in the scale in Part A, add the scores as follows.

Add up scores for statements	Your score	Maximum score		Remarks (Is your score high, moderate, or low?)
Statements: 1 + 2 + 3 + 4 + 5 + 6		30	Self-transcendence through society-benefitting work	6–10 = low; 11–20 = moderate; 21–30 = high
Statements: 7 + 8 + 9 + 10 + 11 + 12		30	Self-transcendence through coworker-benefitting relationships in workplace	6–10 = low; 11–20 = moderate; 21–30 = high
Add up the above two scores		60	Workplace spirituality	12–20 = low; 21–40 = moderate; 41–60 = high

Exercise 1: Questions for reflection on self-assessment of workplace spirituality (Part C)

Note: The first four questions focus on your own experience of workplace spirituality in your work unit or organization, while the subsequent questions focus on the workplace spirituality experienced by most of the employees in your work unit or organization.

1 What is the level of workplace spirituality you experience in your work unit or organization (low, moderate, or high)?
2 How does the existing level of workplace spirituality experienced by you affect your work?
3 How does the existing level of workplace spirituality experienced by you affect you as a human being?
4 What actions can you take to improve your experience of workplace spirituality?
5 What is likely to be the level of workplace spirituality experienced by most of the employees in your work unit or organization (low, moderate, high)?
6 What actions can you take to improve the experience of workplace spirituality for most of the employees in your work unit or organization?

References

Albuquerque, I. F., Cunha, R. C., Martins, L. D. and Britosa, A. 2014. Primary health care services: Workplace spirituality and organizational performance. *Journal of Organizational Change Management*, 27(4): 59–82.

Allen, N. J. and Meyer, J. P. 1996. Affective, continuance, and normative commitment to the organization: An examination of construct validity. *Journal of Vocational Behavior*, 49: 252–276.

Ashmos, D. P. and Duchon, D. 2000. Spirituality at work: A conceptualization and measure. *Journal of Management Inquiry*, 9(2): 134–145.

Bateman, T. S. and Organ, D. W. 1983. Job satisfaction and good soldier: The relationship between affect and employee citizenship. *Academy of Management Journal*, 26: 587–595.

Benefiel, M., Fry, L. W. and Geigle, D. 2014. Spirituality and religion in the workplace: History, theory, and research. *Psychology of Religion and Spirituality*, 6(3): 175–187.

Benson, P. L., Roehlkepartain, E. L. and Rude, S. P. 2003. Spiritual development in childhood and adolescence: Toward a field of inquiry. *Applied Developmental Science*, 7(3): 205–213.

Chakraborty, S. K. 1993. *Managerial Transformation by Values*. Sage: New Delhi.

Chandler, C. K., Holden, C. M. and Kolander, J. A. 1992. Counseling for spiritual wellness: Theory and practice. *Journal of Counseling & Development*, 71: 168–175.

de Klerk, J. J. 2005. Spirituality, meaning in life, and work wellness: A research agenda. *International Journal of Organizational Analysis*, 13(1): 64–88.

Duchon, D. and Plowman, D. A. 2005. Nurturing spirit at work: Impact on work unit performance. *The Leadership Quarterly*, 16: 807–833.

Ellison, C. W. 1983. Spiritual well-being: Conceptualization and measurement. *Journal of Psychology and Theology*, 11(4): 330–340.

Fry, L. W., Vitucci, S. and Cedillo, M. (2005). Spiritual leadership and army transformation: Theory, measurement, and establishing a baseline. *Leadership Quarterly*, 16: 835–862.

Geigle, D. 2012. Workplace spirituality empirical research: A literature review. *Business and Management Review*, 2(10): 14–27.

Giacalone, R. A. and Jurkiewicz, C. L. 2003. Toward a science of workplace spirituality. In R. A. Giacalone and C. L. Jurkiewicz (Eds.), *The Handbook of Workplace Spirituality and Organizational Performance* (pp. 3–28). ME. Sharpe: Armonk, NY.

Grant, A. M., Christianson, M. K. and Price, R. H. 2007. Happiness, health, or relationships? Managerial practices and employee well-being tradeoffs. *Academy of Management Perspectives*, 21(3): 51–63.

Greenberg, J. S. 2002. *Comprehensive Stress Management*. McGraw-Hill: Boston.

Hoffman, B. J., Blair, C. A., Meriac, J. P. and Woehr, D. J. 2007. Expanding the criterion domain: A quantitative review of the OCB literature. *Journal of Applied Psychology*, 92(2): 555–566.

Kinjerski, V. and Skrypnek, B. J. 2006. Measuring the intangible: Development of the Spirit at Work Scale. *Paper Presented at the Sixty-fifth Annual Meeting of the Academy of Management*, Atlanta, GA.

Kolodinsky, R. W., Giacalone, R. A. and Jurkiewicz, C. L. 2008. Workplace values and outcomes: Exploring personal, organizational, and interactive workplace spirituality. *Journal of Business Ethics*, 81: 465–480.

McKee, M. C., Driscoll, C., Kelloway, E. K. and Kelley, E. 2011. Exploring linkages among transformational leadership, workplace spirituality and well-being in health care workers. *Journal of Management, Spirituality and Religion*, 8(3): 233–255.

Milliman, J., Czaplewski, A. J. and Ferguson, J. 2003. Workplace spirituality and employee work attitudes: An exploratory empirical assessment. *Journal of Organizational Change Management*, 16: 426–447.

Milliman, J., Ferguson, J., Trickett, D. and Condemi, B. 1999. Spirit and community at Southwest Airlines. *Journal of Organizational Change Management*, 12: 221–233.

Mirvis, P. H. 1997. 'Soul work' in organizations. *Organization Science*, 8(2): 190–206.

Moberg, D. O. and Brusek, P. J. 1978. Spiritual well-being: A neglected subject in quality of life research. *Social Indicators Research*, 5(3): 303–323.

Paloutzian, R. F., Emmons, R. A. and Keortge, S. G. 2003. Spiritual well-being, spiritual intelligence, and healthy workplace policy. In R. A. Giacalone and C. L. Jurkiewicz (Eds.), *The Handbook of Workplace Spirituality and Organizational Performance* (pp. 123–136). ME. Sharpe: Armonk, NY.

Pawar, B. S. 2014. Leadership spiritual behaviors toward subordinates: An empirical examination of the effects of a leader's individual spirituality and organizational spirituality. *Journal of Business Ethics*, 122: 439–452.

Pawar, B. S. 2009a. Individual spirituality, workplace spirituality and work attitudes: An empirical test of direct and interaction effects. *Leadership & Organization Development Journal*, 30(8): 759–777.

Pawar, B. S. 2009b. Workplace spirituality facilitation: A comprehensive model. *Journal of Business Ethics*, 90(3): 375–386.

Pawar, B. S. 2013. A proposed model of organizational behavior aspects for employee performance and well-being. *Applied Research in Quality of Life*, 8(3): 339–359.

Pawar, B. S. 2016. Workplace spirituality and employee well-being: An empirical examination. *Employee Relations: The International Journal*, 38(6): 975–994.

Pawar, B. S. 2017. The relationship of individual spirituality and organizational spirituality with meaning and community at work. *Leadership & Organization Development Journal*, 38(7): 986–1003.

Petchsawanga, P. and Duchon, D. 2009. Measuring workplace spirituality in an Asian context. *Human Resource Development International*, 12(4): 459–468.

Petchsawanga, P. and Duchon, D. 2012. Workplace spirituality, meditation, and work performance. *Journal of Management, Spirituality & Religion*, 9(2): 189–208.

Petty, M. M., McGee, G. W. and Cavender, J. W. 1984. A meta-analysis of the relationship between individual job satisfaction and individual performance. *Academy of Management Review*, 9(4): 712–721.

Podsakoff, P. M., MacKenzie, S. B., Paine, J. B. and Bacharach, D. G. 2000. Organizational citizenship behavior: A critical review of the theoretical and empirical literature and suggestions for future research. *Journal of Management*, 26(3): 513–563.

Saks, A. M. 2011. Workplace spirituality and employee engagement. *Journal of Management, Spirituality, and Religion*, 8(4): 317–340.

Chapter 9

Reflections on implementation of leadership, justice, support, and workplace spirituality

Enhancing employee performance and well-being

The value of the book's research-based inputs for managerial actions

Thoughtful or planned actions of human beings are based on their knowledge of the world. Acquiring knowledge of the world involves developing beliefs about various aspects of the world. The ways of developing beliefs or knowing include methods of tenacity, authority, intuition, and science (Kerlinger and Lee, 1992, pp. 6–8). Revising and extending this view of Kerlinger and Lee (1992), one can suggest that the ways of knowing include tradition, authority, intuition, experience, and science. A person's knowledge coming from such various sources could shape his/her planned or thoughtful actions. These aspects of how human beings develop knowledge and act based on it can apply to managers as well.

A manager, without the benefit of knowledge coming from the method of science or research-based knowledge, may take actions based on his/her beliefs or knowledge coming from tradition, authority, intuition, and experience. As an example, consider a situation where a manager has to enhance employee performance. If he/she is working for an organization where the tradition has been to demand high employee performance and punish employees for not attaining the demanded performance level, then he/she may use this approach to enhance employee performance if he/she relied on the tradition to know what enhances employee performance. If the manager's superior had told him/her that the best way to enhance employee performance is by providing more financial incentives for higher performance and if the manager was to rely on the authority of his/her superior to know what enhances employee performance, then he/she may promise and provide more financial rewards for higher employee performance levels. If the manager's subconsciously held pattern or intuition tells him/her that high employee performance comes from employees' involvement in performance target setting and if he/she was to rely on his/her intuition, then he/she may provide employees involvement in setting employee performance targets in order to enhance employee performance. If the manager was to rely on his/her own experience of what actions in the past enhanced employee performance and use his/her knowledge coming from past experience, then for enhancing employee performance, he/she may take those actions that, as per his/her past experience, have worked in the past.

All these methods of knowing and actions based on them may have limitations. For example, what worked traditionally may not work at present, the knowledge provided by the authority figure of the manager's superior may not be applicable in the manager's situation, the past events on which the patterns of intuition are developed may not apply to the current events, and the past experience-based knowledge may not hold as a correct guide for actions in the present circumstances. Thus, the approach of a manager using sources of knowledge other than science-based or research-based knowledge to guide his/her actions may have limitations.

Science-based or research-based knowledge provides a distinct knowledge base that a manager can use to guide his/her actions. Using this source of knowledge, a manager can take those actions which research has found to be effective in enhancing employee performance. This research-based knowledge tends to be, to varying extents, objective in the sense of being somewhat free from subjective biases, empirically supported in terms of being reflective of reality rather than hypothetical, and generalizable and hence applicable in a reasonably wide range of situations. Thus, research-based knowledge can facilitate managerial actions by providing knowledge that is distinct from knowledge coming from tradition, authority, intuition, or experience, and research-based knowledge has certain positive features. The preceding chapters have attempted to provide such research-based knowledge for facilitating managerial actions for enhancing employee performance and well-being. This provision of research-based knowledge to facilitate managerial actions may highlight the utility of the book's contents for managerial actions aimed at enhancing employee performance and well-being. Some inputs for implementing the book's core contents are outlined below.

Implementing transformational leadership, organizational justice, organizational support, and workplace spirituality

In light of the description in Chapter 5, for enhancing transformational leadership in an organization, various possibilities can be considered. First, a manager can enhance his/her own transformational leadership. For this, he/she can use the self-assessment similar to the one provided at the end of that chapter to assess his/her present level of transformational leadership and reflect on the possible ways of enhancing his/her practice of specific categories of transformational leadership behaviors. He/she can also attend a transformational leadership training program. Second, a manager could then help, either himself/herself or through the human resources department, the lower level managers in his/her organization to enhance their transformational leadership based on self-assessment and reflection and by providing transformational leadership training for them.

In light of the description in Chapter 6, for enhancing organizational justice, actions will need to focus on each of the three forms of justice – distributive, procedural, and interactional. Of these three forms of justice, interactional justice is likely to be most under the control of a manager. For example, a manager could begin to provide to his/her employees truthful and comprehensive explanations of the constraining circumstances or higher purposes that necessitated certain decisions about the employees. This will enhance employee experience of informational justice, which is a dimension of interactional justice. A manager could also hold and express respect for employees' self-respect and dignity and be polite while providing explanations about employee-related decisions. This will enhance employee perceptions of interpersonal justice, which is a dimension of interactional justice. The human resources department could also conduct training programs to help all managers in the organization to understand the nature, consequences, importance, and ways of enhancing interactional justice. A similar approach could be used for enhancing the other two forms of justice – distributive and procedural. A manager needs to understand, based on the contents of the organizational justice chapter, the features that can enhance these two justice forms and take appropriate actions to implement these features in his/her work unit or organization. Assessing the current level of justice in a work unit or an organization before taking such actions may help in focusing effort on enhancing those forms of justice which are at very low level at present and which therefore need to be enhanced. The self-assessment exercise at the end of the chapter on organizational justice could help in assessing the present justice levels in an organization.

In light of the description in Chapter 7, for enhancing organizational support, a manager needs to behave with subordinates in such a manner that conveys to them that he/she regards their inputs important and is interested in making them happy. Providing benefits to employees that they perceive as being provided discretionarily, and not under compulsion, by the manager or the organization and which can fulfill employees' strong needs is one possible action for a manager. As employee beliefs of organizational support are shaped by how employees are treated by various officials across different situations, (Eisenberger, Huntington, Hutchison, and Sowa, 1986) it is important that all managers in an organization treat employees in a way that conveys to the employee that they value employees' contribution to the organization and are interested in improving employees' well-being. Thus, conducting an organization-wide training program for managers on the nature, consequences, importance, and ways of enhancing employee beliefs of organizational support would be an important step for enhancing employee beliefs of organizational support.

In light of the description in Chapter 8, for enhancing workplace spirituality, a manager could encourage his/her subordinates to enhance their own individual spirituality level. For this, he/she can provide subordinates information on various spiritual development approaches such as meditation, breathing exercises, and mantra chanting. Conducting workshops to provide subordinates with training on these approaches is another possible action. A similar approach could be adopted by the human resources department to enhance individual spirituality of employees in the entire organization. These actions reflect an inside-out approach described in the workplace spirituality chapter. Another possible action is to create organizational conditions that help employees feel that their work is serving society and that they are providing acceptance, understanding, and care to their coworkers in the workplace and help them have the feeling of meaning in work and feeling of community at work. Explaining to employees how their products or services benefit society is one way of enhancing employees' feelings of meaning in work. For example, in a hospital organization, one could explain to nurses and ward assistants in the hospital how their work helps several families have the joy of seeing their beloved family members return home cured from their stay in the hospital. When the nurses and ward assistants understand this positive impact of their work, they will experience meaning in their work, which is a component of workplace spirituality experiences.

Interconnected implementation of transformational leadership, organizational justice, organizational support, and workplace spirituality

Actions to implement transformational leadership, organizational justice, organizational support, and workplace spirituality in an organization are likely to facilitate implementation of each other. For instance, transformational leadership implementation could result in enhanced organizational justice, as research (Pillai, Scandura, and Williams, 1999) has found a positive relationship between transformational leadership and some dimensions of organizational justice. Further, implementation of organizational justice can enhance organizational support, as research (e.g., Moorman, Blakely, and Niehoff, 1998) has found a positive relationship between procedural justice and organizational support. One way of implementing workplace spirituality is through an organization's adoption of spiritual values. Justice is an organizational value characterizing workplace spirituality (Jurkiewicz and Giacalone, 2004). Thus, implementation of workplace spirituality through an organization's adoption of values is likely to enhance organizational justice. Further, transformational leadership is also positively associated with workplace spirituality (McKee, Driscoll, Kelloway, and Kelley, 2011), and thus enhancing one of these two is likely to aid the enhancement in the other. These interconnections between transformational leadership, organizational justice, organizational support, and workplace spirituality suggest that implementing one of these features in an organization is likely to support the implementation of some of the remaining features.

Actions for implementation of transformational leadership, organizational justice, organizational support, and workplace spirituality are also likely strengthen the positive effects of each other. For example, organizational justice is positively associated with employees' trust in their supervisor and organization

(Cohen-Charash and Spector, 2001), and transformational leadership is also associated with subordinates' trust in the leader (Podsakoff, MacKenzie, Moorman, and Fetter, 1990). Thus, actions for implementing transformational leadership and organizational justice to some extent could complement the effect of each other in enhancing employee trust. Further, one of the ways of enhancing workplace spirituality is to get subordinates to do works that serve society or a larger cause. Transformational leadership is positively associated with the subordinates' sense of higher purpose in work (Sparks and Schenk, 2001). Thus, actions to implement workplace spirituality and transformational leadership could complement each other in enhancing employees' feelings of higher purpose in their work. These examples illustrate the possibility that actions for implementing transformational leadership, organizational justice, organizational support, and workplace spirituality are likely to strengthen the positive effects of each other.

A possible underlying theme for implementing transformational leadership, organizational justice, organizational support, and workplace spirituality

Transformational leadership, organizational justice, organizational support, and workplace spirituality each seek to induce employees to go beyond their narrow or material self-interests (Pawar, 2009). Workplace spirituality implementation can help employees to develop a higher level of spirituality. Employees with a high level of spiritual development are likely to look for and feel satisfied with work that contributes to others. Thus, employees with high spiritual development are likely to seek and feel satisfied with meaningful or noble work. Transformational leadership enhances the significance of subordinates' work by creating an attractive vision. Thus, while workplace spirituality can enhance employees' spiritual development and urge to do meaningful work, transformational leadership provides subordinates meaningful or noble work. Transformational leadership also induces employees to go beyond their self-interests (e.g., Bass, 1985). Justice builds trust and social exchange between employees and the organizational authorities and thus can induce employees to exert extra effort for the organization. Organizational support can help employees persist in their effort, because with organizational support, employees will believe that the organization appreciates their efforts and wants to make them happy (Eisenberger et al., 1986). Further, organizational support can also induce in employees to feel an obligation to benefit the organization (e.g., Eisenberger, Armeli, Rexwinkel, Lynch, and Rhoades, 2001), suggesting that employees are likely to go beyond their self-interests to benefit their organization.

Thus, the actions for implementing transformational leadership, organizational justice, organizational support, and workplace spirituality can collectively induce employees to do noble work, provide noble work to employees, motivate employees to trust the organizational authorities, and contribute more effort for the noble tasks provided by the organization. This indicates that these features act through a common mechanism of inducing employees to contribute to something noble by putting in extra effort for the organization.

There are additional mechanisms through which these four actions can enhance both employee performance and well-being. Transformational leadership makes subordinates "more aware of the importance of task outcomes" (Yukl, 1999, p. 286), stimulates subordinates' "higher-order needs" (Sparks and Schenk, 2001, p. 853), and spurs them to "transcend their own self-interests for the good of the group, organization, or society" (e.g., Bass, 1990, p. 53). Thus, subordinates are likely to feel that they are doing a meaningful or noble task and likely to work for it in a self-interest-transcending or noble way. Workplace spirituality, when implemented through changes in organizational features such as having a noble or socially beneficial organizational cause, is likely to provide employees meaning in work by providing them noble work. Workplace spirituality, when implemented through the spiritual development of individual employees, is likely to create an urge in employees to seek meaning through work or to contribute to a noble cause. Thus, workplace spirituality, by developing an urge in employees to do work that is beneficial to others, can induce employees' transcendence beyond material self-interests. Organizational justice can foster trust (e.g., Cohen-Charash and Spector, 2001) and social exchange relationship of an employee with the organization and supervisors (e.g., Masterson, Lewis, Goldman, and Taylor, 2000). In a social exchange relationship between two parties, the parties contribute to each other without expecting immediate and point-for-point trade of commodities. Thus, social exchange between employees and an organization is likely to induce employees to put in more effort for the organization without necessarily expecting immediate material rewards. This is another form in which employees can go beyond their self-interests for the organization. Employee beliefs of organizational support can induce employees to benefit the organization through mechanisms such as reciprocity (Eisenberger et al., 1986) and felt obligation (Eisenberger et al., 2001). Employees' urge to benefit the organization out of felt obligation or reciprocity, rather than for the immediate expected material gain, is a form of employees' self-transcendence.

The common aspect of employees' self-interest-transcendence likely to be induced by transformational leadership, organizational justice, organizational support, and workplace spirituality is noted in Pawar (2009). Thus, actions to implement transformational leadership, organizational justice, organizational support, and workplace spirituality are likely to work in a mutually reinforcing

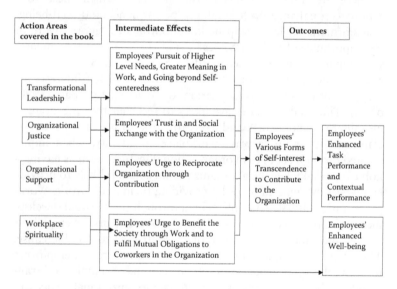

Figure 9.1 The mutually reinforcing outcomes of transformational leadership, organizational justice, organizational support, and workplace spirituality

Note: The "Intermediate Effects" depicted are partly based on various works including Bass (1985), Bass (1990), Eisenberger et al. (1986), Eisenberger et el. (2001), Masterson et al. (2000); Pawar (2009), and Sparks and Schenk (2001). For the links of transformational leadership, organizational justice, organizational support, and workplace spirituality with other components of this figure, citations to some of the associated literature works and descriptions are provided in the preceding chapters on these four topics and also in Chapters 3 and 9.

way to induce employees' self-transcendence for the organization and to generate a high level of employee performance. This mutually reinforcing nature and a possible sequence of processes likely to be activated by transformational leadership, organizational justice, organizational support, and workplace spirituality are presented in Figure 9.1.

Implementation of transformational leadership, organizational justice, organizational support, and workplace spirituality with other approaches

Some of the traditional approaches such as goal setting, employee participation, and job enrichment were described in Chapter 4. Some of these and other approaches can be implemented along with transformational leadership, organizational justice, organizational support, and workplace spirituality. These all can facilitate enhancement in employee performance and well-being as depicted in Figure 9.2.

Some examples of implementing other organizational behavior interventions with the action areas from the book are as follows. Job enrichment and goal-setting can be used as employee-oriented practices to create features in the job that can contribute to higher performance and well-being. Similarly, employee participation can be used to create a more inclusive work context for employees. Further, workplace spirituality can enhance the individual spirituality of the leader, can facilitate spiritual values in an organization, and can provide a vision of service to an organization. Transformational leadership can also provide a vision of service to an organization. Implementation of transformational leadership, organizational justice, organizational support, and workplace spirituality can establish employee-oriented practices in an organization. Thus, traditional organizational behavior interventions such as job enrichment, goal-setting, and employee participation can be used along with the action areas outlined in this book to enhance employee performance and well-being.

The actions outlined in this chapter are provided only as examples. Based on the contents of earlier chapters and this chapter, a manager can design several actions for enhancing employee performance and well-being in his/her organization. From the contents of the first three chapters, a manager will be clear about the

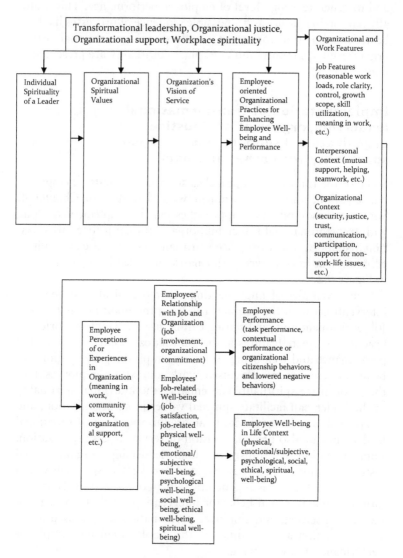

Figure 9.2 How leadership, justice, support, and workplace spirituality can be applied with other organizational behavior interventions

Source: Reproduced and adapted with permission from Pawar (2013, p. 349)

nature of employee performance and well-being and their importance for the effectiveness of his/her organization. From the contents of Chapter 5 to Chapter 8, a manager will become aware of the key aspects of transformational leadership, organizational justice, organizational support, and workplace spirituality and also of how making improvement in these in his/her organization can enhance employee performance and well-being. To facilitate reinforcement of this understanding and application of this understanding through action planning, exercises at the end of each of these four chapters (Chapters 5, 6, 7, and 8) will help a manager understand the present level of transformational leadership, organizational justice, organizational support, and workplace spirituality in his/her organization and will also help him/her to identify possible actions for improving the levels of these features in his/ her organization. Thus, from the chapters preceding this chapter, a manager will be in a position to identify actions for improving transformational leadership, organizational justice, organizational support, and workplace spirituality in order to enhance employee performance and well-being. In addition to these action-facilitating inputs from the preceding chapters, the contents from this chapter provide some illustrations to help a manager to systematically approach the task of developing actions for improving transformational leadership, organizational justice, organizational support, and workplace spirituality in order to enhance employee performance and well-being. Further, this chapter provides the contents that add a new dimension to how a manager could design interrelated actions for improving transformational leadership, organizational justice, organizational support, and workplace spirituality to enhance employee performance and well-being. This chapter also provides the contents that add could help managers develop clarity about how interrelated actions for improving transformational leadership, organizational justice, organizational support, and workplace spirituality can work through complementary processes for enhancing employee performance and well-being.

In conclusion, the first three chapters provided inputs on the nature, importance, and forms of employee performance and well-being. The four chapters immediately preceding this chapter provided inputs on the nature, importance, processes, and outcomes associated with transformational leadership, organizational justice, organizational support, and workplace spirituality. This chapter described how the research-based knowledge included in the preceding chapters could help managers access a knowledge base beyond other sources such as tradition, authority, intuition, and experience. This chapter also described how the contents of the book could help managers implement transformational leadership, organizational justice, organizational support, and workplace spirituality and how the implementation of these could have mutually reinforcing effects in enhancing employee performance and well-being.

References

Bass, B. M. 1985. *Leadership and Performance Beyond Expectations*. Free Press: New York, NY.

Bass, B. M. 1990. *Bass & Stogdill's Handbook of Leadership*. Free Press: New York, NY.

Cohen-Charash, Y. and Spector, P. E. 2001. The role of justice in organizations: A meta-analysis. *Organizational Behavior and Human Decision Processes*, 86(2): 278–821.

Eisenberger, R., Armeli, S., Rexwinkel, B., Lynch, P. D. and Rhoades, L. 2001. Reciprocation of perceived organizational support. *Journal of Applied Psychology*, 80: 42–51.

Eisenberger, R., Huntington, R., Hutchison, S. and Sowa, D. 1986. Perceived organizational support. *Journal of Applied Psychology*, 71: 500–507.

Jurkiewicz, C. L. and Giacalone, R. A. 2004. A values framework for measuring the impact of workplace spirituality and organizational performance. *Journal of Business Ethics*, 49: 129–142.

Kerlinger, F. N. and Lee, H. B. 1992. *Foundations of Behavioral Research*. Cengage Learning: Belmont, CA.

Masterson, S. S., Lewis, K, Goldman, B. M. and Taylor, M. S. 2000. Integrating justice and social exchange: The differing effects of fair procedures and treatment on work relationships. *Academy of Management Journal*, 43(4): 738–748.

McKee, M. C., Driscoll, C., Kelloway, E. K. and Kelley, E. 2011. Exploring linkages among transformational leadership, workplace spirituality and well-being in health care workers. *Journal of Management, Spirituality and Religion*, 8(3): 233–255.

Moorman, R. H., Blakely, G. L. and Niehoff, B. P. 1998. Does perceived organizational support mediate the relationship between procedural justice and OCB. *Academy of Management Journal*, 41(3): 351–357.

Pawar, B. S. 2009. Some of the recent organizational behavior concepts as precursors to workplace spirituality. *Journal of Business Ethics*, 88: 245–261.

Pawar, B. S. 2013. A proposed model of organizational behavior aspects for employee performance and well-being. *Applied Research in Quality of Life*, 8(3): 339–359.

Pillai, R., Scandura, T. A. and Williams, E. A. 1999. Leadership and organizational justice: Similarities and differences across cultures. *Journal of International Business Studies*, 30(4): 763–779.

Podsakoff, P. M., MacKenzie, S. B., Moorman, R. H. and Fetter, R. 1990. Transformational leader behaviors and their effects on followers' trust in leader, satisfaction, and organizational citizenship behaviors. *Leadership Quarterly*, 1(2): 107–142.

Sparks, J. R. and Schenk, J. A. 2001. Explaining the effects of transformational leadership: An investigation of the effects of higher-order motives in multilevel marketing organizations. *Journal of Organizational Behavior*, 22: 849–869.

Yukl, G. 1999. An evaluation of conceptual weaknesses in transformational and charismatic leadership theories. *Leadership Quarterly*, 10(2): 285–305.

Index